CONTE

PREFACE

When I decided to put together this collection, I was surprised to find that no other anthology of Irish nationalist writings was available. Irish nationalism has a rich tradition. Most of these names will likely already be familiar to an Irish reader, but they will know them for their actions more than their words. These are figures that dedicated their lives to the cause of Irish nationalism. Some gave their lives. All thought deeply about their struggle, their nation and its place in history. It is a great shame that the Irish nation has neglected this body of thought and turned some of these men into mere footnotes in our historical struggle, for their writings have lost no relevance or insight to the passage of time.

This work covers the period of the first emergence of revolutionary Republicanism in the 1790s to the beginnings of the Gaelic Revival a century later. Originally, I planned this to be a single volume, encompassing the whole history of Irish nationalism. It was putting together the work of the thinkers in this volume, encompassing the 18th and 19th Centuries, that I realised the output of these men was worthy of its own work.

This is the century where the foundations of a real independence movement were laid. Irish nationalism went from a fleeting revolutionary impulse into a sustained movement that blended political, cultural, and militant strands, laying critical foundations for the truly national independence struggle of the 20th century. In many ways, this is the bleakest period in Irish history: encompassing the failed 1798 Rebellion, the subsequent Act of Union in 1801 which fully incorporated Ireland into the United Kingdom, and The Great Famine. As such, the overall tone of this period oscillates between despair and resilience. Yet despite the hardship throughout this century, there was a trend of growing organisation, defiance, and self-confidence found through national figures like Daniel O'Connell, Charles Stewart Parnell, and the cultural revivalists.

By 1900, Irish nationalism stood poised for the revolutionary leaps ahead, its roots deepened by a century of struggle. This volume profiles the men who carried the torch of Irish freedom in some of her darkest hours, when the nation faced unprecedented repression, humiliation and death. Their idealism and resilience in the face of these often dire circumstances make their written word more impactful. These are not just the musings of theoreticians and ideologues, but the living testament of individuals who saw beyond the chains of their era to a future where Ireland might stand sovereign and proud.

In compiling these writings, *An Cartlann* has proved an invaluable resource.[1] I also wish to thank my friend Aaron, who helped in suggesting which works to include.

April 2025

---

[1] cartlann.org

INTRODUCTION

Human settlement in Ireland began around 8000 BC, during the Mesolithic period, after the retreat of Ice Age glaciers. Archaeological evidence indicates that small groups of hunter-gatherers arrived by sea from Britain or western Europe. These early inhabitants relied on fishing, hunting, and gathering, establishing temporary camps that left little impact on the archaeological record. Their population remained small, limited by the resources available on the small island, until the Neolithic period introduced significant change.

By 4000 BC, farming communities arrived, replacing and blending with earlier hunter-gatherers. Coming to Ireland from Britain and continental Europe, these settlers brought domesticated animals, cereal crops, and pottery. They constructed megalithic structures, including Ireland's iconic passage tombs like Newgrange and Knowth in the Boyne Valley, proof of complex ritual practices and organised societies. This migration established Ireland's first substantial population base, laying the groundwork for later demographic shifts.

The Bronze Age, beginning around 2500 BC, saw another major population movement associated with the Bell Beaker culture, which most likely took the form of a violent invasion. Named for their distinctive bell-shaped pottery vessels, the Bell Beaker culture likely originated in Iberia. As well as their distinctive pottery, they brought with them advanced metalworking and mining techniques, leaving traces like the copper mines at Mount Gabriel in County Cork. Their impact is perhaps most striking in their burial practices, seen at Tara, where single inhumations replaced earlier traditions. At this sacred site, archaeologists have uncovered individual graves containing bodies carefully interred with grave goods like pots and jewellery, signalling a new reverence for personal status and the afterlife. This kind of burial practice is a marker of Indo-European peoples, and the Bell Beaker culture was one successor to the so-called "Yamnaya culture" of the early Proto-Indo-Europeans. Genetic studies show a significant influx of new Steppe-related DNA entering Ireland during this period, reflective of a transformative migration of Indo-European people.

This new population wave, peaking around 2400 BC, coincides with a near-complete replacement of the earlier Neolithic gene pool in Ireland, suggesting that this ancient invasion almost completely displaced the prior Neolithic populations, who were likely no match for the expansive Bronze Age warriors. The Bell Beaker arrival totally reshaped Ireland's population and material culture. It provided the genetic stock of the island that has changed little since, isolated from other major population movements on the continent. This population transformation also brought an expansion of trade networks, connecting Ireland to a wider Bronze Age culture in Britain and the continent.

It is with the Iron Age, starting around 600 BC, that we see the introduction of Celtic culture to Ireland, evident in the spread of La Tène-style artifacts such as iron tools and hillforts. It was once believed this cultural shift was brought by a Celtic invasion of Ireland, but we now know there was in fact a very stable continuity with earlier Bronze Age populations, showing little sign of a major new influx. Instead, it seems Ireland's native inhabitants adopted Celtic language and practices through cultural diffusion, likely coming via elites who encountered Celtic culture through trade and contact with Celtic-speaking regions in Britain. It was in this period that the Irish Gaelic language emerged as dominant, giving the island's inhabitants a more distinct cultural identity. Ireland had always been divided politically, with sovereignty fragmented among many local chieftains governing small kingdoms or túatha. Yet by the Iron Age there was a distinct people and language in Ireland that would change little up to the modern period.

The adoption of Celtic culture was one major part of the creation of what is distinctively Irish culture, another was the arrival of Christianity in the fifth century AD. St. Patrick, a British-born missionary, is responsible for this conversion from paganism. Patrick, captured as a slave in Ireland before returning as a missionary, established churches and converted local leaders, achieving a full-scale religious conversion of the island. The shift integrated Ireland into the wider Christian world, yet also reinforced its cultural distinctiveness, for unlike in Roman Britain, Christianity in Ireland blended much more with existing customs to create a distinctive Celtic Christianity. Monasteries adopted a decentralised structure that mirrored the túatha system. St. Patrick was revered in Irish tradition not just as a propagator of the Gospel, but also as a legitimiser of native traditions he deemed compatible with Christianity, blessing the pre-Christian Brehon Law of Ireland. In the centuries that followed, monastic hubs like Clonmacnoise became beacons of Gaelic learning, blending local traditions with Latin scholarship and helping cement a cultural cohesion around Irish identity.

During the early Middle Ages, these monasteries became renowned centres of scholarship not just in Ireland, but across the

Christian world, attracting students and scholars from all over Europe and establishing Ireland as a pivotal centre of education in the Latin world. Their emphasis on manuscript illumination and the preservation of classical texts helped sustain and spread knowledge during a time when most of the rest of the continent faced cultural decline. But for Ireland it was a golden age culturally, in which it earned the affectionate title of 'the land of saints and scholars', and in which Irish monks produced some of the finest artefacts of medieval Christian art in the form of high crosses and illustrative manuscripts like the renowned Book of Kells.

Politically, Ireland remained fragmented, but the concept of the High King (Ard Rí) reflects an early sense of an Irish political unity. Dating back to at least the fifth century, the High King was a ceremonial overlord, claiming authority over regional kings from the sacred site of Tara. Medieval Irish literature portrayed an unbroken line of High Kings ruling Ireland from the Hill of Tara that stretched back thousands of years. In practice, this title was contested, with rival dynasties like the Uí Néill in the north and the Eóganachta in the south vying for dominance. The Annals of Ulster and other texts record these struggles, showing that while the High King lacked centralised power, the existence of the position symbolised a shared aspiration for unity. Although this is something quite distinct from modern idea of nationalism, it does indicate a recognition of Ireland as a single entity, even if this was always tenuous politically.

Beginning in the late eighth century, Ireland became a centre of the Viking Age. Norse raids began targeting Ireland's rich monasteries and other settlements, before Vikings established permanent settlements like Dublin, Wexford, and Waterford by the ninth century. These coastal enclaves introduced trade and urbanism, linking Ireland to existing Scandinavian networks. The Vikings came as hostile invaders, but over time they often assimilated, adopting the native language and intermarrying with the native population. The Norse presence also intensified regional conflicts, as local kings often chose to ally with them over their regional enemies.

The tenth and eleventh centuries saw efforts to assert greater political control over all of Ireland, exemplified in the rise of Brian Boru. A member of the Dál Cais dynasty from Munster, Brian challenged Uí Néill dominance, consolidating power through military campaigns and alliances. In 1002 AD, Brian claimed the High Kingship of Ireland. Inspired by Julius Caesar, he styled himself *Imperator Scottorum*: Emperor of the Irish. His victory at the Battle of Clontarf in 1014 AD against a combined Viking and Leinster force cemented his legacy, though he was killed in the battle. Brian's death fragmented his coalition, and no successor ever matched his scope. But his reign did mark a symbolic peak in the idea of Irish unity, drawing on Gaelic traditions and Christian legitimacy to project a proto-national vision, even if it remained yet unrealised.

Norman rule in Ireland began in 1169, initiated by the invitation of Diarmait Mac Murchada, King of Leinster. Led by Richard de Clare (Strongbow), the Normans brought their distinctive feudalism, today most visible in the many Norman castles dotted around Ireland. Initially allies of local rulers, they soon established lordships, particularly in Leinster. As with the Norse invasions, over time many Anglo-Normans assimilated, adopting Gaelic customs and language and marrying into the native population. The English Crown, alarmed by the trend, imposed the Statutes of Kilkenny in 1366 which banned settlers from speaking Irish or marrying natives. However, the statutes had little impact, and the Hiberno-Normans continued to assimilate to the dominant Irish cultural identity. Outside of The English Pale, an area encompassing modern Dublin and surrounding areas, Gaelic and Norman-Irish lords retained a great deal of autonomy from the British crown. This period solidified a dual identity: a native Irish core, now Christian and Irish speaking, alongside a partially integrated foreign elite.

The sixteenth century marked a turning point with the Tudor conquest, as England sought to impose centralised authority over all of Ireland. Henry VIII declared himself King of Ireland in 1541, introducing the "surrender and regrant" policy, which required Gaelic lords to submit to English rule in exchange for retaining their lands under feudal titles. Many complied formally but preserved traditional practices, limiting the policy's effectiveness and still frustrating the British Crown's desire to fully entrench British rule over Ireland. The Reformation, initiated by Henry and enforced under Elizabeth I, only deepened divisions. Most Irish rejected Protestantism, in large part because of its association with English dominance, meaning that Catholicism emerged as a marker of resistance and became more central to Irish identity.

The persecution of Catholicism also forced closer alliances between many of the "Old English" who had maintained their Catholic faith and now felt greater affinity with their Irish neighbours. Better educated than the native Irish, many became great opponents of the reconquests of Ireland from the Tudor era on. One example is the historian Geoffrey Keating, born to a Gaelicised Old English family in Tipperary in 1580. Keating was termed 'the Herodotus of Ireland' for gathering old Irish manuscripts and oral traditions and ordering and archiving them to safeguard their existence from the collapse of the old Gaelic tradition. The culmination of this project was his major work, *Foras Feasa ar Éirinn* (The History of Ireland), which became widely popular among the educated in Ireland and led to a stronger sense of a shared national identity.

Elizabeth I's reign saw military efforts to suppress opposition, including the Desmond Rebellions (1569–1583) and the Nine Years' War (1594–1603). The latter, led by Irish lords Hugh O'Neill and Hugh Roe O'Donnell, was a serious blow at English power in Ireland. The Irish confederacy drew in thousands of fighters, captured most of the island, secured a string of military victories, and secured military aid from Catholic Spain. However, the English secured a vital victory at the battle of Kinsale in 1601, turning the course of the war. The Flight of the Earls in 1607, when O'Neill and other leaders fled to Europe (after news of another planned rebellion reached British authorities) signalled the final collapse of the political order of Gaelic Ireland. The Plantation of Ulster followed, beginning in 1609, with land confiscated from Catholic owners and granted to Protestant settlers from England and Scotland.

The seventeenth century further solidified English control. In response to ongoing land dispossession by an increasingly aggressive Protestant regime, the 1641 Rebellion saw Gaelic Irish and Old English Catholics unite against the encroaching Protestant settlers. The Catholic rebels managed to seize two thirds of the country, with Royalist forces only holding Dublin, Cork and surrounding areas, with some Protestant militias holding parts of Ulster. Out of the captured territory, the rebels formed the Irish Catholic Confederation, with its government based out of Kilkenny. Irish self-government over so much of the territory of Ireland, and reports of atrocities committed against Protestant settlers, prompted a severe response in the form of Oliver Cromwell's conquest of Ireland, beginning in 1649.

The result of Cromwell's brutal campaigns was a demographic shock — as much as 20% of the Irish population died in this period to war, famine and plague — and a drastic reduction in Catholic land ownership to the benefit of Protestant settlers. The Penal Laws, introduced after the Williamite War (1689–1691), restricted Catholics and non-Anglican Protestants from political participation, landownership, and education. These measures established the Protestant Ascendancy, a minority ruling class aligned with Britain, which generated widespread and longstanding discontent among the excluded population. By this stage, Irish identity began to reflect more a shared experience of subordination and resistance, as the many failed attempts of the native Irish to break the English yoke creating, through generations, a romantic canon of Irish nationalist struggle.

In the eighteenth century, Ireland functioned as a subordinate kingdom within the British system, governed by a Dublin Parliament that served the Ascendancy's interests. Economic policies restricted trade, and the Penal Laws continued to marginalise Catholics and Presbyterian Dissenters. The native Irish, reduced to tenant farmers, faced growing hardship, while the Old English Catholic gentry had also lost influence. In Ulster, Presbyterians, though Protestant, encountered discrimination from the Anglican establishment, fostering resentment. The Enlightenment brought ideas of popular sovereignty and individual liberty to the educated in Ireland, as well as a spirit of revolutionary zeal, influencing young idealists in urban centres like Dublin and Belfast. The American Revolution's success in removing British rule further inspired Irish nationalists. The Irish Volunteers, formed in 1778 as a militia, became a political force, securing the Constitution of 1782, which increased parliamentary autonomy. However, this body remained under British control and excluded non-Anglicans, failing to address broader grievances.

The Society of United Irishmen, founded in 1791 in Belfast by figures like Theobald Wolfe Tone, emerged in this environment. The group drew on French Revolutionary ideals, but initially sought peaceful parliamentary reform, including an expansion of the vote and Catholic emancipation. It aimed to unite Ireland's religious communities under a shared national struggle against British rule. It was here that the Irish national struggle became wedded to the ideals of Republicanism, a political ideal under which the country would eventually unite for its national independence struggle in the 20th century. But this was just the political form — by this time, there was a clearly distinct Irish people, culture and identity with roots stretching back to the ancient world.

From the Mesolithic hunter-gatherers who first tread its shores to the Gaelic-speaking Christians who resisted centuries of conquest, Ireland's story is one of resilience. Across millennia, waves of migration, cultural diffusion and differentiation, foreign incursion and resistance forged a unique people with a rich culture. The Tudor conquest and subsequent English domination hardened this identity, binding it to Catholicism and a romantic yearning for the ideal of an Ireland both Gaelic and free. The eighteenth and nineteenth century's revolutionary fervour crystallised these threads into a more distinctly modern nationalist vision which, carried by the bravery and sacrifice of one of Ireland's most heroic generations, would achieve the victories that began the end of British rule in Ireland.

The United Irishmen

Our collection begins at the end of the 18th century, when British rule was firmly entrenched in Ireland. The Penal Laws, beginning in the seventeenth century, had institutionalised a system of oppression which stripped Catholics of land, rights, and political representation. In the eighteenth century, some notable Protestant patriots like Jonathan Swift and Henry Grattan began to chafe at Ireland's subjugation within the British Empire. Grattan's Parliament of 1782 was a limited victory for legislative independence, but it still excluded the Catholic majority which fuelled simmering discontent.

It was against the backdrop of suppressed Gaelic traditions, Catholic disenfranchisement, and minority Protestant disillusionment that the United Irishmen arose. They were not merely heirs to the legacy of Irish national resistance, but also political innovators in their time. They weaved together Ireland's existing sense of unity and cultural pride with a revolutionary Republican ideology inspired by the American and French revolutions. Unlike earlier movements, often confined to one religious or social faction, the United Irishmen sought to bridge sectarian divides, drawing Dissenters from Ulster, Catholics from the countryside, and enlightened Protestants from the cities into a shared cause under an Irish flag.

In reality though, their leadership – consisting of men like Theobald Wolfe Tone, James Napper Tandy, and Thomas Russell – was overwhelmingly Protestant and from the major urban centres of Belfast and Dublin. The organisation began as a peaceful, reformist society intended to agitate for annual parliaments and a non-sectarian propertied manhood franchise. It gradually became more militant in the 1790s, influenced by the French revolution and in response to unexpectedly harsh British repression. Wolfe Tone himself first favoured constitutional reform, but after a crackdown which drove the group underground, became convinced that only a full-scale violent rebellion could achieve Irish independence.

Included here is Wolfe Tone's *Address To The People Of Ireland*, a rallying cry to the militant Republicanism that would become intertwined with the national idea for the next two centuries. Included also, is Robet Emmet's *Speech From The Dock*, given in a Dublin courtroom just before he was sentenced to death. The speech not only inspired future nationalists with its spirit of heroic sacrifice and defiance, but has come to be universally recognised as one of the finest pieces of oration ever. It was also, somewhat ironically, the likely inspiration for Winston Churchill's "We shall fight on the beaches" speech, now perhaps the most famous piece of oration ever.

The 1798 Rebellion of the United Irishmen failed, and immediately after was regarded as a disaster by the masses of Ireland, leading to the Act of Union and final dissolution of the Irish parliament for full union with Britain. It was two generations later, that another generation of young idealists began to rehabilitate and romanticise the noble sacrifice of the United Irishmen. Although their uprising failed, the United Irishmen's gallant sacrifice would become the inspiration for another, more successful generation of revolutionaries.

Address to the People of Ireland

Wolfe Tone

At length the time is arrived when a friend to the Liberty and Independence of Ireland, may venture to speak the truth, and examine into the situation and interest of his country, without fear of being stopped short by that most unanswerable of all arguments, an information in the Court of King's Bench, at the suit of his Majesty's Attorney General.

It is long since every honest Irishman has mourned in secret over the misery and degradation of his native land, without daring to murmur a syllable in the way of complaint. Not even our groans were free! Six hundred years of oppression and slavery have passed in melancholy succession over our father's heads and our own, during which period we have been vilified by every evil, which tyranny could devise and cruelty execute; we have been scattered, like chaff, over the land, and our name has been forgotten among nations; we have been massacred and plundered, insulted and despised; we have been reduced to that lowest state of human degradation; we have almost ceased to respect ourselves; we have doubted whether the opinion of our oppressors was not just, and whether we were not in fact, framed for that submission, to which we have been bent by the pressure of so many centuries of hand, unremitting, unrelenting tyranny.

But if the judgements of Providence be slow, they are certain. The villain must not hope to walk in credit to his grave, nor the tyranny to insult for ever, with impunity, the misery, he has caused. The pride and arrogance of England have at length called down upon her head the tardy and lingering justice, which her manifold crimes have so long provoked; the sufferings of Ireland, prostrate and humble as she has been, even to the dust, seem to have awakened the attention of him, who rules the destiny of nations; in his goodness and compassion he has at length regarded us, and placed in our hands the means, if we have the courage to be free.

Without being too much of an enthusiastic visionary, I think I may say I see a new order of things commencing in Europe. The stupendous revolution, which has taken place in France; the unparalleled succession of events, which have, in defiance of the united efforts of all the despots of Europe, established that mighty republic on the broad and firm basis of equal rights, liberties, and laws; the abasement, contrary to all human probability, of her enemies, every one of whom has, in his turn, been forced to yield to her ascendant genius, with the exception thus far, of Austria, and especially England, whose fall has only been delayed, to make her degradation more terrible, and the triumph of her victorious rival the more complete; all this, I say, has satisfied my mind, that the ancient system of tyranny must fall. In many nations it is already extinct, in others, it has received its death wound, and though it may for some time trail a feeble and lingering existence, its duration is ascertained, and its days already numbered. I do not look upon the French revolution as a question subject to the ordinary calculation of politics; *it is a thing which is to be*; and as all human experience has verified that the new doctrine ever finally subverts the old; as the

Mosaic law subverted idolatry, as Christianity subverted the Jewish dispensation, as the Reformation subverted Popery, so, I am firmly convinced, the doctrine of Republicanism will firmly subvert that of Monarchy, and establish a system of just and rational Liberty, on the ruins of the Thrones of the Despots of Europe.

But whether this opinion be well or ill founded, the question I mean to examine will not be affected by the result. Fortunately or unfortunately for Ireland, her cause is independent of the theory. The object for her immediate consideration, is not whether she shall adopt this or that form of Government, but whether she shall be independent under any. She has too many solid, substantial, heavy, existing grievances, to require much ingenuity, or subtle argument, to convince her of her interest and her duty, and the question on which we must take an instant determination will, if I mistake not, be decided as soon as it is stated.

The alternative which is now submitted to your choice, with regard to England is, in one word, UNION OR SEPARATION! You must determine, and that instantly, between slavery and independence, there is no third way. I will not insult you, by doubting what will be your decision. I anticipate your immediate and unanimous declaration, which establishes for ever Liberty to yourselves, and Independence to your country.

To a magnanimous people it is unnecessary to prove that it is *base*, to an enlightened people it is unnecessary to prove that it is *ruinous*, to exist in dependence on the will of a foreign power, and that power an ambitious rival. To you this is not matter of mere speculation – you feel it in your government, in your laws, in your manners, in your principles, in your education; with all the great moral and physical advantages, of which you are possessed, you are unnoticed and unknown as a nation in Europe; your bodies and your minds are bent down by the incumbent pressure of your tyrant; she, to maintain whose avarice and ambition you are forced to spill your best blood, in whose cause you fight without glory, and without profit, where victory but rivets your chains the faster, and where defeat adds to slavery, mortification and disgrace. In vain are you placed in the most advantageous position for unlimited commerce, in vain are you blessed with a fruitful foil, with every requisite for trade and manufactures, with inexhaustible mines, with navigable rivers, and with the noblest harbours in Europe. All these advantages are blasted by the contagious presence of your imperious rival, before whose influence your strength is withered, your resources crushed, and the rising spirit of emulation strangled in the birth. It is England, who debauches and degrades your gentry; it is England, who starves your manufacturers, to drive them into her fleets and armies; it is England, who keeps your wretched peasantry half-fed, half-clothed, miserable and despised, defrauded of their just rights, as human beings, and reduced, if the innate spirit of your country did not support them, as it were by a miracle, below the level of the beasts of the field; it is England who buys your legislators, to betray you, and pays them by money levied on yourselves; it is England, who forments and perpetuates, as far as in her lies, the spirit of religious dissension among you, and that labours to keep asunder Irishman from Irishman, because that in your cordial Union among yourselves, she sees clearly the downfall of her usurpation, and the establishment of your liberties; it is England, who supports that rotten, aristocratic faction among you, which, though not the tenth part of your population, has arrogated to itself five-sixths of the property, and the whole of the patronage and power of your nation; a faction which to maintain itself by the power of England, is ready to sacrifice, and does daily sacrifice your dearest rights to her insatiable lust of gold power.

Look to the origin of your connection with Britain, that proud and selfish nation, and see what is the foundation of the authority of your oppressors! Six hundred years ago, the Pope, an Englishman, thought proper to confer the crown of Ireland on Henry the 2d, King of England; and the King of England was pleased in return to guarantee to his countryman, the Pope, the payment of a certain tax *to be levied on the People of Ireland*; but were the People consulted, whose liberties and properties were thus bartered away between these two Englishmen? No such thing – their independence was sold by one foreigner to the other, without their privity or concurrence, and to consummate the injustice of this most infamous and audacious bargain – they were compelled themselves to raise the purchase money of their disgrace, *and to pay for being enslaved*. Such was the commencement of the British Monarchy in Ireland, and what have been its fruits? Six hundred years of continual intestine wars, marked with every circumstance of horror and barbarity, with the desolation of whole provinces, with massacres and confiscation and plunder, with fire, famine and pestilence, with murder to that horrible extent, that at length it was decreed, even by your own Legislature, to be no crime in an Englishman to kill *a mere Irishman*. When by these multiplied abominations; your strength was exhausted, and your spirit broken; when your oppressors made it their boast that you were *brayed as it were in a mortar*, this execrable tyranny of the sword was succeeded by the still more execrable tyranny of laws, framed with a diabolical sagacity to impoverish and degrade and brutalize you; laws even yet but imperfectly removed, and for whole partial repeal, extorted from your reluctant oppressors, you are indebted to the recent union among yourselves, to your consequent spirit, and to the combination of events produced by the French Revolution.

But to compensate you for the loss of your independent existence as a nation, for the destruction of your trade and manufactures, the plunder of your property, the interdiction of education, to three-fourths of your People, and their absolute exclusion from a state of political existence, you have been gravely told that you participated in what is called in the cant of your enemies, *the inestimable blessings of the British Constitution.*

I will not here enter into the merits or demerits of that Constitution. You have read the productions, which have appeared on that subject, and it is therefore unnecessary for me to repeat them; on him, who is not convinced by the arguments of Payne, of the absurdity of hereditary monarchs, and hereditary legislators, where no man would admit of hereditary cobblers, who wished to have his shoes well-mended, I despair of making any impression, I will therefore for the sake of argument suppose, though I will by no means admit, that this Constitution is really as excellent as it is represented to be by its warmest panegyrists, who, by the bye, will ever be found amongst those who exist by its daily destruction, and I answer, in the first place, that you may, if you choose, adopt that Constitution as your own, when your independence is once recognized, and you come to organise your Government; but to quit this, which I look upon as a wild and idle supposition, I say in the second place, that you do not possess this excellent and happy Constitution! that, even in England, it is disfigured and distorted, but that in Ireland it is so smothered beneath a mass of corruption, as to be, in effect, no more the Constitution of England, as it exists in theory, than it is the Constitution of Constantinople or Japan.

In the first place what is your King? Your King is a foreigner, an Englishman, a native of a country, that holds you in utter contempt; whom you never see nor expect to see; who never condescends to visit Ireland, who, with all the ignorant prejudices and illiberal passions of his nation, distributes from his closet at St. James's, by the advice of the British Cabinet, the honours and rewards of your country, either among English sycophants, or more despicable Irish apostates, whose strongest recommendation to his royal favour, is that they are ready at all times, and without scruple, to sacrifice the interest and independence of their native land to the avarice or ambition of England. Is there a man of you, that is not convinced, and that has not felt, that even the meanest Englishman considers himself as your superior, and despises an Irishman in his heart? And have you not had a thousand occasions to know that the King of England holds as rank and vulgar prejudices on that score as the lowest and most ignorant of his vassals? That he regards you, not as a nation of valuable subjects, but as a rabble of mutinous slaves, and that your whole realm is not of as much importance in his eyes as any one manufacturing town of England. People of Ireland, this is your *absentee* Monarch! This is the idol, before whom you are to fall down, and to worship, like another Moloch, with the sacrifice of your blood; to pamper whose pride and folly and ambition, you are daily called upon to devote your treasures and your lives, your individual liberties, and the glory and independence of your native land; and this is the sentiment, which is called loyalty by those, who wish to deceive and to mislead in order that they may plunder and oppress you.

But perhaps you find in the national spirit, in the patriotism and virtue of the other two estates of your Legislature, the Lords and the Commons, a protection from the ruinous effects of an Executive power, deposited in a foreign country, connected with you by no ties of interest or of glory, actuated solely by selfish motives, and illiberal prejudices, and who is represented by a fugacious personage, bound by no responsibility and amenable to no tribunal.

See then the redoubtable barrier against oppression, which you have in your House of Lords! In the very first instance one half of them are Englishmen, who never saw Ireland, who have not a foot of property there, who do not think it worth their while even to visit the country, from which they derive their titles, but who would of themselves be sufficient to stifle all opposition by their numbers, if those noble Lords, who are in the habit of attending Parliament were to be found, miraculously, in opposition to the mandate of the British Minister. The means, by which a peerage is obtained in Ireland, and the motives which determine the King of England, *the fountain of honour*, to raise his faithful subjects to that high rank, are of sufficient notoriety. It is well known, and has been asserted even in your Parliament, that the honours of the peerage are prostituted to the most infamous purpose of corruption; that they are bought and sold in open market, and at a stated price, or made a subject of a more ruinous, though less disgraceful commerce, in debauching the other branch of the Legislature; that sometimes a man is made a peer, because he can command two votes in the House of Commons, and sometimes because he can command five thousand pounds in money; sometimes because he has been obedient as a judge in trials, where the Crown has been concerned, and sometimes because he has been refractory in Parliament, and it is necessary to appease him. If there were any reason to expect a possibility of patriotism or public virtue from a body thus constituted, there are six and twenty bishops, many of them Englishmen, and all of them expectants of the English Government for promotion or translation, ready to strangle it in the birth. Such are the hereditary counsellors of the Crown in Ireland, the judges in the last resort, the impartial and incorruptible guardians of the Constitution, against the encroachments of the people on the one side, and the King on the other; the people, with whom they have no common interest, and the King, who names the peerage and episcopacy, who distributes ribands and Stars, and mitres, and places and pensions, at his pleasure.

The Crown and the Lords being thus organized against you, and having confessedly their own distinct and separate interests to consult, at least it is hoped that the third estate, the Commons, your representatives, emanating from yourselves, deriving their existence from the choice of the people, of which they make a part, surely they at least will take care of your rights, your liberties, and your interest, which are their own; proud of the sacred deposit, which you have confided in their hands, they will magnanimously resist any attempt of the other two estates, should any such be made, to invade the inalienable privileges of their constituents; amenable to the tribunal of your opinion, they will dread the disgrace invariably attached to corruption in a Legislator, even more than death; should any courtly pander be found hardy enough to risqué the attempt to debauch their stern integrity, they will turn aside from his presence with horror and disgust, if indeed the first emotion of insulted virtue does not rather prompt them to seize the villain, to drag him from his den to public view, and denounce him to the nation as the most atrocious to all parricides, the assassin of his country.

I cannot continue this irony! the subject is too sorrowful to excite any other feeling than indignation. Who are these abominable slaves, so impudently called your representatives? How are they chosen? Who are their constituents? It is not so notorious as no longer to excite surprise, or scarcely resentment, that the most inestimable of our privileges, from which all others depend, the right to choose your Legislators is made a daily subject of a base and villainous traffic? That a station the most honourable to which man can aspire, that of representing his fellow-citizens in the great council of the nation, is bought and sold, and that feats in Parliament are become a subject of dirty, commercial speculation; so that any fellow, even of the most infamous character, provided he can raise three thousand pounds, may in defiance of the public indignation and contempt, place himself triumphantly on the benches of your Legislature, and make laws to bind millions of men, any one of whom would scarcely trust himself alone in his company, or suffer him to enter his house, without previously locking up his spoons. The Temple of your liberties is filled with buyers and sellers, with money changers and thieves; with placemen and pensioners; those unclean and ominous harpies, gorged with the public spoil, and sucking still, like insatiable Vampires, the last drainings of the vital blood of their country; with fraudulent bankrupts, who take shelter in Parliament from the persecution of their creditors, and purchase with a part of their plunder, the privilege to retain the rest in security; with speculating lawyers, who, without principles and without practice, and destitute of talents to rise in their own profession, take up the more gainful trade of making in the Legislative those laws, which in the courts they are unable to expound, force on their way with inveterate perseverance, a servility that knows no scruple, and imprudence incapable of a blush, repel their abler and honester brethren, who can not bend to those vile means of advancement, and make a short cut through Parliament to the judgement-feat; with those miserable automations, the humble dependants of great men, who place them as their puppets in the House of Commons, and whose condition is, I know not whether more to be pitied or despised; with young coxcombs of fortune, who think *a feat in the House*, like their whores, their horses, and their hounds, a necessary appendage to their rank and dignity; even the members for your counties, where, if at all, the public voice might be supposed to have some little influence, even in their election, a system of corruption universally prevails, less compendious than that, which exists in your boroughs, but more scandalous and destructive. I do not fear that any one man in Ireland, even on your Treasury bench will be found, with a forehead hard enough to deny one syllable of what I have here advanced, or even to assert that the picture is overcharged. Your Parliament has long lost all character, as it has lost all decency; every honest man despises it; the prostitutes, who compose it know this and tremble; in vain do they multiply laws for their protection, and persecute without remorse the slightest invasion of what they are pleased to vote to be their privileges; the sanction of character is wanting; the public opinion is pronounced against them, and nothing but the pressure of an incumbent force has prevented the indignant spirit of Ireland, from bursting forth long since, and levelling with the dust the edifice of her oppression.

From a Legislature, constituted as yours is, no good can flow. Those who compose it, have no common interest with the people – they feel that they are but a foreign colony, depending entirely for their existence on the connection with England, whose power alone secures them in possession of their usurpation. If they had the inclination (of which I am far from suspecting them) they have not the courage to be honest. The fact and truth is, that the great bulk of the aristocracy of Ireland, conscious that their estates were originally acquired by the most unjustifiable means, either by open robbery, sword in hand, or by the more infamous pillage of the laws, dare not oppose the will of the British Minister, from the apprehension lest he should withdraw his protection from their party, and leave them to the mercy of the majority of their countrymen. It is vain to argue with men under the influence of so extreme a fear. Those of them, who are more enlightened, and who, of course, do not dread a resumption of property, which the lapse of time, and a change of circumstances, have rendered impossible, yet affect a terror they do not feel, to confirm the delusion of the rest, and profit of the panic, which in a great degree they have themselves caused, and diligently cultivated, to govern their party, and to perpetuate their monopoly in every department of the state. By these means they are enabled to make their bargain with the British Minister, and nothing can be imagined less difficult than the negotiation. Their language is simply this –

"Maintain us in our places, our pensions, and our power; suffer us to support our mistresses, our dependants, and ourselves, at the public expense; surrender to us, in a word, the entire patronage of the crown; in return we engage to surrender to you the commerce, the manufactures, the liberty and the independence of Ireland; we will support you in every measure, which you may devise, to impoverish, to divide, and to weaken our country; we will abet you in every mad and ruinous war, in which you may think proper to embark; we will squander the blood of Ireland, without limitation or reserve; *we will stand and fall with England*; suffer us only in return to appropriate to ourselves such portion of the public treasure as the sacrifices we may make to you may appear to deserve."

To a proportion so just and reasonable in itself, it is not to be supposed the English Minister can be so captious as to raise the least objection. He purchases, in fact, for England every advantage she can possibly derive from the connection between the countries, without putting her to the expense of sixpence, for Ireland, who is sold, is also forced to raise the purchase money; and herein lies the essential difference between the political situation of England and Ireland. In the former undoubtedly the Constitution is depraved and degraded, and corruption carried on to an enormous extent; the liberty of the people is, beyond contradiction, sacrificed to the arbitrary will and pleasure of the King; but at the same time their essential interests are, in all other respects, consulted by the Government. The Minister there studies to advance their trade and manufactures, by all possible means, justifiable, and unjustifiable, upon the same principle that the farmer manures the soil he means to cultivate, and feeds the beast he destines for labour. Under this point of view I have no hesitation to admit that England is essentially well and wisely governed, and a mere merchant or manufacturer, who looks no further than his warehouse or his shop, has no reason to wish for a change. But do you, my countrymen, lay your hands on your hearts, and ask yourselves, *is all this so with us?* I do not fear contradiction when I answer for you that the direct contrary is the fact, and that your legislators are *hired* and *paid* by the English Minister, (paid with your own money I beseech you to keep ever in memory) to destroy and smother your arts, manufactures and commerce in the cradle, lest they might by possibility interfere with the interest of England, who will be ever undoubtedly, better pleased to see you a colony of idlers, to consume her manufactures, and to recruit her fleets and armies, than to meet you in the markets of the world, an active, enterprising, and industrious rival. No English Minister would have the folly or the impudence to propose to the corrupt and profligate of his dependants a measure subversive of the interests of the nation, or if he were so utterly infatuated, which is indeed impossible, he would not be a Minister for four and twenty hours after. When a member of Parliament in England sells himself, it is always with a saving clause; there are things he will not do, and which he never will be asked to do; but a member of Parliament in Ireland who sells himself (as they all do, or wish to do) is, politically speaking, damned without reserve; the condition of his bargain is to surrender his country to the mercy of England. I do not here speak of your liberties, for in that respect the people of England are nearly as badly off as yourselves, but in the name of God, consider how this connection affects your interests, and see how absolutely and utterly different your condition is from theirs, in that respect. The commerce of England is protected and cherished and fostered by the Government; on a question of trade, all consideration of party vanishes, every man, whatever be his political delinquency, is alike eager to forward any measure which promises to be beneficial, and even the most abject slaves in the English House of Commons, are honest upon that score. But how is it with prostitutes of the Irish House of Commons? The indispensable requisite, the fundamental principle of their bargain, I repeat it, is the sacrifice of their country to the avarice and ambition of England. I appeal with confidence to your own unvarying experience, to determine whether in Ireland there be any road to preferment, other than an implicit deference to the will of the English Minister. Is any man promoted, or will any man ever be promoted to power or station, at least while the connection holds, because he is, or is even suspected to be the friend of his country? Would not such a suspicion operate infallibly to his exclusion? And hence it is, that it is impossible under the present system, that you can ever have an honest Government, because the English Minister, who names your rulers, will be sure to exact from them such conditions and engagements as no honest Irishman can by possibility submit to, and consequently none but knaves and sycophants, who are ready without scruple to take this abominable covenant, can fill place or office; it is not so in England, because there, as I have already said, the essential interests of the nation are equally the object of all parties, and a man may accept a situation in the Government, without sacrificing his integrity or his reputation; but I defy any man to take a share in the measures of the Irish Government, without a total surrender of all principle and character, as an Irishman. Number, I beseech you, your tyrants; consider the most virulent of your oppressors, man by man; review the whole of their political career, and see what are the means whereby they have become your rulers. Have they any other merit than that of blind submission to the will of England, a profligate eagerness to sacrifice the very existence of Ireland to her arbitrary will and pleasure? Turn then to those, who call themselves your patriots, and see whether they are not essentially as much your enemies, and as ready to prostrate you and themselves at the feet of your tyrants, as the most impudent and abandoned of her acknowledged hirelings. Do you not go to your Legislature, as to a comedy, to be amused by the talents of the actors, well knowing the part which each is to play, and what is to be the catastrophe of the piece? Can you not, on every question of importance, before hand with precision how every individual will vote, and upon what motives? Do you believe, on your honour and conscience, that you could find ten men in your entire Legislature, who act upon conviction or principle? Is not making your laws, as much a trade as making your shoes, and not the thousandeth part so honest or so respectable? And if all this be so, what kind of Administration is that under which you groan, for a brave, a sagacious and an enlightened people with warm hearts, with quick feelings, and with strong resentments?

But I waste time in dwelling on grievances, and abuses, which you all know and feel. The difficulty in enumerating the sufferings of Ireland is not what to choose, but what to reject; so many abominations crowd at once on my mind, and every one more atrocious than the other. Let me turn from a subject so disgusting in all points of view, as your actual Government, and contemplate the brilliant prospect which lies before us, the promised land of liberty and happiness, to secure the possession of which, we have but to act with the spirit of men, and to profit of the great occasion, which Providence has at length afforded us. We have now the means, in the first place, to break that execrable slavery, by which, under the more plausible name of connection, we have been chained for six hundred years at the feet of England; we have in our hands independence for our country, the first blessing of nations, and liberty for ourselves, without which life is not worth preserving; we shall no longer be dragged perpetually from the line of our obvious interests, by the overbearing attraction of our tyrant, nor forced to run and prostrate

ourselves at the feet of an English Minister, to obtain his permission
to regulate the concerns of our country? The aristocracy of Ireland,
which exists only by our slavery, and is maintained in its pomp and
splendour by the sale of our lives, liberties, and properties will
tumble in the dust; the People will be no longer mocked with the vain
appearance of a Parliament, over which they have neither influence
or control. Instead of a King, representing himself, a House of Lords
representing themselves, and a House of Commons representing
themselves, we shall have a wise and honest Legislature, chosen by
the People, whom they will indeed represent, and whose interest,
even for their own sakes, they will most strenuously support. Our
commerce will be free, our arts encouraged, our manufactures
protected, four our enemies will no longer be our law-makers. The
benches of our Legislature will no longer groan under the load of
placemen and pensioners, the hirelings of a foreign power, and the
betrayers of our country; we shall have upright Judges to administer
the laws, for the road to the judgement-feat will no longer be through
the mire of Parliamentary corruption; we shall have honest Juries to
determine on our liberties, properties and lives, for the Crown will
no longer nominate our Sheriffs, on the recommendation of this or
that grandee; the host of useless offices, multiplied without end for
the purposes of corruption, will be annihilated, and men will be
made hereafter for places, and not places for men; the burdens of the
people will be lightened, for it will be no longer the custom to buy
majorities in Parliament; the taxes, which will be hereafter levied,
will be honestly applied to the exigencies of the State, the regulation
of commerce, the formation of a Navy, the making of roads, the
cutting canals, the opening of mines, the deepening our harbours,
and calling into activity the native energy of the land. Instead of the
state of daily suicide wherein Ireland now exists, her resources will
at length be actively employed for her interest and her glory.
Admission to the Legislature will be no longer to be purchased with

money, and the execrable system of jobbing, so long our disgrace and ruin, will be forever destroyed, the trade of Parliament will fail, and your borough-mongers become bankrupts. Your peasantry will be no longer seen in rags and misery, their complaints will be examined, and their sufferings removed; instead of the barbarous policy which has so long kept them in want and ignorance, it will be the interest as well as duty of national Government to redress their grievances and enlighten their minds. The unnatural union between Church and State, which has degraded Religion into an engine of policy, will be dissolved, tithes the pest of agriculture will be abolished, the memory of religious dissensions will be lost when no sect shall have a right to govern their fellow-citizens, each sect will maintain their own Clergy, and no citizen shall be disenfranchised for worshipping God according to his conscience. To say all in one word, IRELAND SHALL BE INDEPENDENT. We shall be a Nation not a Province; Citizens not Slaves. Every man shall rank in the State according to his merit and talents. Our commerce shall extend into the four quarters of the globe, our flag shall be seen on the ocean, our name shall be known among the nations, and we shall at length assume that station, for which God and Nature have designed us.

I feel that I am proving an axiom. Can any honest man for a moment doubt that an independent nation will better regulate her own concerns than if she was subjugated to another country, whose interest it is to oppress her? I will therefore assume as a fact, that independence is an object of the highest possible advantage to Ireland, and I will briefly consider what are the weighty motives, for weighty indeed they must be, which have thus long induced her to forego so great a blessing and to remain in humble subjection to England.

The first and most striking, and in fact the true reason, is the dread of risking a contest with a power, which we are habituated to look upon as our superior. Every man agrees that independence is a good thing, if it could be had, but dreads to hazard the little he enjoys in surety for the speculation of a great benefit, the acquisition of which is remote, and attended with uncertainty and danger.

Not to dwell upon the pusillanimity of this mode of reasoning, the first answer I have to give is conclusive. It is no longer a matter of choice; we must take our party on the instant and decidedly; we have now all we wanted; allies, arms, and ammunition, stores, artillery, disciplined troops, the best and bravest in Europe, besides the countless thousands of our brave and hardy peasantry, who will flock to the standard of their country. The sword is drawn, the Rubicon is passed, and we have no retreat; there remains now no alternative; if we were even inclined, we could not return to the state, in which we were three months ago. We must conquer England and her adherents, if any yet she has among ourselves, or they will conquer us, and then *vae victis*! To the brave and honest majority of my countrymen, who are ready to sacrifice their lives for the independence of Ireland, I do not now address myself; but to those timid and cautious speculators, who may hang back, and wait upon contingencies, and fluctuate and balance before they choose their party, to such men, and I hope at this glorious period, few such will be found, I appeal; and I desire them, even for their own sakes, to consider that in a war like that, wherein we are now engaged, there is no neutrality; we fight for our liberties, dearer far than life, and in such a contest he that is not with the people, is against them; him we do not find in our ranks, we must hold as an enemy, and an enemy in the highest degree, a deserter and a traitor, to his country. If any man dreads the issue of the contest, it is notwithstanding the interest as it is the duty, of even that man to come forward in the defence of the common cause, for it is only in the possibility of disunion among ourselves, that England can form the slightest hope of success in the contest.

If she sees all ranks and descriptions of Irishmen united and determined, she will balance, after the experience of America and France, before she will engage in a third crusade against the liberties of an entire nation. The sure way to avert the calamities of war from our country is to show we are to a man resolved to face them with courage; or if war must be, the infallible means to insure its speedy and glorious termination, is to bring to bear on our enemy the consolidated force of the Irish nation. In the present crisis, it is therefore the interest even of the most cautious man to step forward in the cause of his country; unless he prefers to sacrifice his property, his honour, perhaps his existence to his fears, for I again repeat it, *In a war for our liberties, we can admit of no neutrality.*

A generous mind is not deterred from a glorious pursuit, because it is attended with danger. It is our duty to hazard every thing when the object is the independence of our native land, were our enemy more powerful than she has been described, or we have been used to conceive her. But let us approach this gigantic figure, by which we have been so long kept in awe and see whether our apprehension, as well as the artifice of our oppressors, have not magnified the object of our fears. The English fleet is very formidable, but we have little commerce, and during the short continuance of the war, we can dispense with it; a shot from a ship will not kill a man a quarter of a mile from the shore, and we have no occasion to go upon the seas to meet them. But either I am much deceived, or it will be found that so far from England being formidable by her fleet, it is there she will be found most vulnerable. Who are they, who man her vessels? TWO-THIRDS OF THEM ARE IRISHMEN; and will those brave and gallant fellows, thousands of whom have been pressed, and the rest driven by famine into her service, will they, I say, be ready to turn their arms against their native land, against their fathers, their brothers, their wives, their children and their friends? It is not to be supposed; besides that we have in our hands the means to secure their co-operation in the glorious contest wherein we are engaged, and in due season it will be seen that we want neither the skill nor the spirit to employ them.

What I have said of the navy applies, in a great degree, to the army of England; if she is determined to make war upon us, she will not venture to do it with the native troops, for there are too many Irish in the ranks; she must therefore do it with foreign mercenaries, if she can find the means to land them; but the mercenaries are not to be had without money, and I entreat you to consider what will be the effect of a war with Ireland upon her finances. Four hundred millions of debt is no slight burden, and the British Minister may not always find lenders. It is no secret that he is, at this moment, in considerable difficulty, and I take it for granted we shall not be so mad as to part with a shilling of English property, until our liberty is established; but supporting he can even find money, money will not do every thing, the gold of Carthage did not save her from the iron of Rome, and I doubt whether in the present contest, the Bank paper of England will be found more efficacious.

But granting she is formidable, so are we; if she is near us, we are near her; our people are brave, and hardy, and poor; we are not debauched by luxury and sloth; we are used to toil, and fatigue, and scanty living; our miseries, for which we have to thank England, have well prepared us to throw off the yoke. We can dispense with feather-beds, with roast-beef, and strong-beer; war, if it makes any change in the diet of our peasants, must change it for the better; they may in that case taste meat and bread, delicacies to them, and which a great majority of them seldom see; our soil and our climate we can well support; we can sleep in our bogs, where our enemies will rot, and subsist on the mountains, where they will starve. We might upon principle and for our liberties; they fight, because they are ordered to do so. We are at home; they are in an enemies' country. Under these circumstances, and especially with a just and righteous cause, he must be timid indeed, who could doubt of success.

England, with Ireland at her back, is undoubtedly formidable; England, with Ireland neuter, is still respectable, but England with Ireland in arms against her, I do not despair of feeling humbled with the dust. Add to what I have said, the discontents which exist, even in her own bosom, and which every years continuance of the war will increase; remember the state of Scotland two years since, and judge whether she may not seize the present great occasion, and like ourselves assert her ancient independence; see the mighty French Republic, Spain, and Holland united against her and friendly to Ireland, and then decide which of us has most to dread from the other.

I leave this point, the discussion of which is only necessary for timid souls, and I come to another, addressed to those of a more generous stamp. It may be said we are indebted to England for protection from our enemies, and that we are of course bound in gratitude and honour, not to desert her in the hour of difficulty. If this argument were founded in fact, I should be ashamed to offer a syllable against it, for with nations, as with individuals, I esteem honour the first of all objects, and no consideration of convenience or interest should be suffered for an instant to stand against it. But, in God's name, who are the enemies, against whom we are protected by England? With what one nation on Earth have we a shadow of difference? Of what people existing have we reason to complain, except England herself? It is true, indeed, that by this baneful connection, which in a thousand shapes presents itself for the destruction of our interests, we have dragged, as reluctant parties into every war, wherein ambition or avarice induces her to embark; we are forced to forego, for the time, the modicum of commerce we possess, we are loaded with taxes, our people are pressed for seamen or lifted for soldiers to fight the battles of England, in the event of which we have no possible interests, unless indeed it be our interest to be defeated, for the prosperity of England has always been the depression of Ireland. In this very war, which she has in her pride and folly waged against the French Republic, we have supplied not less than two hundred thousand of our gallant countrymen to combat against our most essential interests; and this is the protection for which we are to be grateful! If a man sets my house on fire first, even though he should afterwards succeed in extinguishing it, am I to be grateful to such a man! If a man drags me into a quarrel for his own interests, and wherein I have nothing to do, am I to thank him, even though by our joint exertion I escape with my life after receiving a sound beating, and losing a great part of my property? See then whether the protection of England differs in any respect from the cases I have just mentioned. The truth and fact is, it is we that protect England; it is our provisions that victual her navy, it is our seaman who man her fleets, and our soldiers, who fill her armies; this is solid, substantial protection, and now that we are at last about to separate from her, for ever, she will soon experimentally feel, to her irrecoverable loss, which of the two nations it is that has thus long protected the other.

Independent of the consideration that this argument is a cowardly one (for what Irishman, or Irishwoman, would, in the hour of danger, seek shelter under the arm of an Englishman!) it involves a gross fallacy, inasmuch as it presumes that without the protection of England we could not exist. It is true that at his hour we have not a navy, neither should we ever have one to the end of time, if the connection with England should so long continue; but the moment that our independence is established, and the resources of our country applied, not to debauch and corrupt \our rulers to sacrifice our dearest interests, but to cherish and bring out the inborn energy of the land, we shall soon see an Irish navy on the ocean, we shall look for protection only to God, and our own courage. We have means far beyond those of half the independent states of Europe, of Denmark, of Sweden, of Portugal, of Naples, of Sardinia. Who at this hour protects America? Who protects Switzerland? The common interest of Europe protects the one, the valour of her people the other. We unite in our case both circumstances. When we have once broken the yoke of England, do not believe that the maritime powers will ever see us return to bondage; if even our own means were insufficient for our protection (which I will never admit), we should speedily find allies; and I presume there is hardly to be found an Irishman, who so little respects his country, or himself, as to doubt that with her own resources, and the assistance of France, Spain, and Holland, Ireland is abundantly competent to her own protection.

There is only one argument more, which suggests itself to my mind, in support of our dependence upon England, and that is, that the condition of Ireland is, latterly, much improved, and therefore we should not desire a change.

I admit our condition is improved, and why? In 1779, when England was embarrassed by her frantic crusade against America, we extorted from her necessities the extension of our trade this was a great improvement, but is it the connection with England we are to thank for that? So far from it, that the first improvement in our condition was the step we then made towards independence. In 1782 we broke another, and a weighty link of the chain, which bound us to England, by establishing an exclusive right of Legislature for ourselves; this was also a great improvement in our condition, inasmuch as it placed us a step farther from England; we had then the means to be honest, if our Legislators had the inclination, and if we have not profited by the advantage, we then obtained, to its full extent, it is because we yet remained too near our enemy, and one end of our chain was still in the hands of the despot of England.

In 1793, when she was on the point of embarking in her second crusade against France, the union of the Dissenters and Catholics took place, and three millions of Irishmen were restored, in a great degree, to their rights; this was the last great improvement in our condition, and of the very highest importance, for by making us at length one people, it has enabled us, if it be not our own faults, to throw off the yoke for ever. Thus it appears that every step that we have made towards independence, has in the same degree bettered our condition; that we have become prosperous as we have become free; that while we were bound close to England, we were poor and oppressed; that in proportion as we have receded from her baneful influence, we have risen nearer to our proper level. I am ready therefore to allow this argument of the increasing prosperity of Ireland its full force, but I drew therefrom a conclusion very different from those, who advance it as a reason for our remaining in subjection to England – for I say that if the imperfect shadow of independence, which we have enjoyed for the last seventeen years, has produced, as all parties will acknowledge it has, such beneficial effects, what may we not expect from a full and complete enjoyment of actual, national independence, when the pressure of our ancient tyrant is once removed, and we are left at liberty to regulate our own concerns, to study our own interests, to cultivate our means, to augment our resources, to profit of our natural advantages, in a word, to bring into play all the latent energy of our country, *"that noble and neglected island, for which God has done so much, and man so little!"*

Look, I beseech you, to America! See the improvement in her condition since she nobly asserted her independence, on a provocation which, when set beside your grievances, is not even worthy to be named. Before the struggle she too was flourishing in a degree far beyond what you have ever experienced; England too was then infinitely more formidable in every point of view than at this hour; but neither the fear of risking the enjoyments she actually possessed, nor the terror of the power of her oppressors, prevented America from putting all to the hazard, and despising every consideration of convenience or of danger, where her liberty was at stake; she humbled her tyrants at her feet, and see how she has been rewarded! Contemplate the situation of America before her independence, and see whether every motive, which actuated her in the contest, does not apply to you with tenfold force; compare her laws, compare her government with yours, if I must call that a government; which is indeed a subversion of all just principle, and a total destruction of the ends, for which men submit to be controlled, and see whether it is not worth the struggle, to place yourselves in a situation, equally happy as hers for yourselves and your friends, and ten times more formidable for your enemies.

I have now done, my countrymen, and I do most earnestly beseech you, as Irishmen, as citizens, as husbands, as fathers, by everything most dear to you, to consider the sacred obligation that you are called upon to discharge, to emancipate your country from a foreign yoke, and to restore to liberty yourselves and your children; look to your own resources, look to those of your friends, look to those of your enemies; remember that you must instantly decide; remember that you have no alternative between liberty and independence, or slavery and submission; remember the wrongs you have sustained from England for six hundred years, and the implacable hatred, or still more insufferable contempt which, even at this moment, she feels for you; look at the nations of the earth emancipating themselves around you. If all this does not rouse you, then are you indeed what your enemies have long called you, A BESOTTED PEOPLE! You have now arms in your hands, turn them instantly on your tyrants; remember, if this great crisis escapes you, you are lost for ever, and Ireland will go down to posterity, branded with the infamy, of which the history of the world has hitherto, for the honour of human nature, furnished but *one instance*. The Cappadocians had once the offer of liberty, they rejected it, and returned to their chains! Irishmen! Shall it be said that you furnish the second, and more disgraceful instance? No, my countrymen, you will embrace your liberty with transport, and for your chains you will *break them on the heads of your oppressors*; you will show for the honour of Ireland, that you have sensibility to feel, and courage to resent, and means to revenge your wrongs; one short, one glorious effort, and your liberty is established. NOW OR NEVER; NOW, AND FOR EVER.

Speech from the Dock

Robert Emmet

Dublin, 19 September 1803

"What have you, therefore, now to say why judgment of death and execution shall not be awarded against you according to law?"

What have I to say why sentence of death should not be pronounced on me, according to law? I have nothing to say which can alter your predetermination, not that it would become me to say with any view to the mitigation of that Sentence which you are here to pronounce, and by which I must abide. But I have that to say which interests me more than life, and which you have laboured, as was necessarily your office in the present circumstances of this oppressed country to destroy. I have much to say why my reputation should be rescued from the load of false accusation and calumny which has been heaped upon it. I do not imagine that, seated where you are, your minds can be so free from impurity as to receive the least impression from what I am about to utter. I have no hope that I can anchor my character in the breast of a court constituted and trammelled as this is. I only wish, and it is the utmost I expect. that your lordships may suffer it to float down your memories untainted by the foul breath of prejudice, until it finds some more hospitable harbour to shelter it from the rude storm by which it is at present buffeted.

Were I only to suffer death, after being adjudged guilty by your tribunal, I should bow in silence, meet the fate that awaits me without a murmur; but the sentence of the law which delivers my body to the executioner, will, through the ministry of the law, labour in its own vindication to consign my character to obloquy, for there must be guilt somewhere—whether in the sentence of the court, or in the catastrophes posterity must determine. A man in my situation, my lords, has not only to encounter the difficulties of fortune, and the force of power over minds which it has corrupted or subjugated, but the difficulties of established prejudice. The man dies, but his memory lives. That mine may not perish, that it may live in the respect of my countrymen, I seize upon this opportunity to vindicate myself from some of the charges alleged against me. When my spirit shall be wafted to a more friendly port—when my shade shall have joined the bands of those martyred heroes, who have shed their blood on the scaffold and in the field in defence of their country and of virtue, this is my hope—I wish that my memory and name may animate those who survive me, while I look down with complacency on the destruction of that perfidious government which upholds its domination by blasphemy of the Most High—which displays its power over man as over the beasts of the forest—which set man upon his brother, and lifts his hand, in the name of God, against the throat of his fellow who believes or doubts a little more or a little less than the government standard—a government which is steeled to barbarity by the cries of the orphans and the tears of the widows which it has made.

Lord Norbury— *"The weak and wicked enthusiasts who feel as you feel are unequal to the accomplishment of their wild designs".*

I appeal to the immaculate God—I swear by the Throne of Heaven, before which I must shortly appear—by the blood of the murdered patriots who have gone before me—that my conduct has been, through all this peril, and through all my purposes, governed only by the convictions which I have uttered, and by no other view than that of the emancipation of my country from the superinhuman oppression under which she has so long and too patiently travailed; and I confidently and assuredly hope that, wild and chimerical as it may appear, there is still union and strength in Ireland to accomplish this noblest enterprise. Of this I speak with the confidence of intimate knowledge, and with the consolation that appertains to that confidence, think not, my lords, that I say this for the petty gratification of giving you a transitory uneasiness. A man who never yet raised his voice to assert a lie will not hazard his character with posterity by asserting a falsehood on a subject so important to his country, and on an occasion like this. Yes, my lords, a man who does not wish to have his epitaph written until his country is liberated will not leave a weapon in the power of envy, nor a pretence to impeach the probity which he means to preserve, even in the grave to which tyranny consigns him.

Lord Norbury — *"You proceed to unwarrantable lengths, in order to exasperate or delude the unwary, and circulate opinions of the most dangerous tendency, for purposes of mischief".*

Again I say that what I have spoken was not intended for your lordship, whose situation I commiserate rather than envy—my expressions were for my countrymen. If there is a true Irishman present, let my last words cheer him in the hour of his affliction—

Lord Norbury— *"What you have hitherto said confirms and justifies the verdict of the jury".*

I have always understood it to be the duty of a judge, when a prisoner has been convicted, to pronounce the sentence of the law. I have also understood that judges sometimes think it their duty to hear with patience, and to speak with humanity; to exhort the victim of the laws, and to offer, with tender benignity, their opinions of the motives by which he was actuated in the crime of which he was adjudged guilty. That a judge has thought it his duty so to have done, I have no doubt; but where is that boasted freedom of your institutions—where is the vaunted impartiality, clemency, and mildness of your courts of justice, if an unfortunate prisoner, whom your policy, and not your justice, is about to deliver into the hands of the executioner, is not suffered to explain his motives sincerely and truly, and to vindicate the principles by which he was actuated?

My lords, it may be a part of the system of angry justice to bow a man's mind by humiliation to the purposed ignominy of the scaffold; but worse to me than the purposed shame or the scaffold's terrors would be the shame of such foul and unfounded imputations as have been laid against me in this court. You, my lord, are a judge; I am the supposed culprit. I am a man; you are a man also. By a revolution of power we might change places, though we could never change characters. If I stand at the bar of this court and dare not vindicate my character, what a farce is your justice? If I stand at this bar and dare not vindicate my character, how dare you calumniate it? Does the sentence of death, which your unhallowed policy inflicts upon my body, also condemn my tongue to silence and my reputation to reproach? Your executioner may abridge the period of my existence, but, while I exist, I shall not forbear to vindicate my character and motives from your aspersions; as a man to whom fame is dearer than life, I will make the last use of that life in doing justice to that reputation which is to live after me, and which is the only legacy I can leave to those I honour and love, and for whom I am proud to perish.

As men, my lord, we must appear on the great day at one common tribunal, and it will then remain for the Searcher of all hearts to show a collective universe who was engaged in the most virtuous actions or actuated by the purest motives—my country's oppressor, or—

Lord Norbury— *"Stop, sir! Listen to the sentence of the law"*.

My lord, shall a dying man be denied the legal privilege of exculpating himself in the eyes of the community from an undeserved reproach thrown upon him during his trial, by charging him with ambition, and attempting to cast away for a paltry consideration the liberties of his country? Why did your lordship insult me? Or rather, why insult justice in demanding of me why sentence of death should not be pronounced? I know, my lord, that form prescribes that you should ask the question. The form also presumes the right of answering. This, no doubt, may be dispensed with, and so might the whole ceremony of the trial, since sentence was already pronounced at the Castle before your jury were empanelled. Your lordships are but the priests of the oracle. I submit to the sacrifice; but I insist on the whole of the forms.

Lord Norbury— *"You may proceed, sir"*.

I am charged with being an emissary of France. An emissary of France! And for what end? It is alleged that I wish to sell the independence of my country; and for what end? Was this the object of my ambition? And is this the mode by which a tribunal of justice reconciles contradictions? No; I am no emissary.

My ambition was to hold a place among the deliverers of my country—not in power, not in profit, but in the glory of the achievement. Sell my country's independence to France! And for what? A change of masters? No; but for my ambition. Oh, my country! Was it personal ambition that influenced me? Had it been the soul of my actions, could I not, by my education and fortune, by the rank and consideration of my family, have placed myself amongst the proudest of your oppressors? My country was my idol. To it I sacrificed every selfish, every endearing sentiment; and for it I now offer myself, O God! No, my lords; I acted as an Irishman, determined on delivering my country from the yoke of a foreign and unrelenting tyranny, and from the more galling yoke of a domestic faction, its joint partner and perpetrator in the patricide, whose reward is the ignominy of existing with an exterior of splendour and a consciousness of depravity. It was the wish of my heart to extricate my country from this doubly-riveted despotism—I wish to place her independence beyond the reach of any power on earth. I wish to exalt her to that proud station in the world which Providence had destined her to fill. Connection with France was, indeed, intended, but only so far as mutual interest would sanction or require.

Were the French to assume any authority inconsistent with the purest independence, it would be the signal for their destruction. We sought their aid— and we sought it as we had assurances we should obtain it—as auxiliaries in war, and allies in peace. Were the French to come as invaders or enemies, uninvited by the wishes of the people, I should oppose them to the utmost of my strength. Yes! My countrymen, I should advise you to meet them on the beach with a sword in one hand and a torch in the other. I would meet them with all the destructive fury of war, and I would animate my countrymen to immolate them in their boats before they had contaminated the soil of my country. If they succeeded in landing, and if forced to retire before superior discipline, I would dispute every inch of ground, raze every house, burn every blade of grass; the last spot on which the hope of freedom should desert me, there would I hold, and the last of liberty should be my grave.

What I could not do myself in my fall, I should leave as a last charge to my countrymen to accomplish; because I should feel conscious that life, any more than death, is dishonourable when a foreign nation holds my country in subjection. But it was not as an enemy that the succours of France were to land. I looked, indeed, for the assistance of France; I wished to prove to France and to the world that Irishmen deserved to be assisted—that they were indignant at slavery, and ready to assert the independence and liberty of their country; I wished to procure for my country the guarantee which Washington procured for America—to procure an aid which, by its example, would be as important as its valour; disciplined, gallant, pregnant with science and experience; that of allies who would perceive the good, and polish the rough points of our character. They would come to us as strangers, and leave us as friends, after sharing in our perils, and elevating our destiny. These were my objects; not to receive new taskmasters, but to expel old tyrants. And it was for these ends I sought aid from France; because France, even as an enemy, could not be more implacable than the enemy already in the bosom of my country.

Lord Norbury— *"You are making an avowal of dreadful treasons, and of a determined purpose to have persevered in them, which I do believe, has astonished your audience".*

I have been charged with that importance in the efforts to emancipate my country, as to be considered the keystone of the combination of Irishmen, or, as your lordship expressed it, "the life and blood of the conspiracy". You do me honour overmuch; you have given to a subaltern all the credit of a superior. There are men engaged in this conspiracy who are not only superior to me; but even to your own conception of yourself, my lord; men before the splendour of whose genius and virtues I should bow with respectful deference, and who would think themselves disgraced by shaking your bloodstained hand—

Lord Norbury— *"You have endeavoured to establish a wicked and bloody provisional government"*.

What, my lord! shall you tell me, on the passage to the scaffold, which that tyranny, of which you are only the intermediary executioner, has erected for my murder, that I am accountable for all the blood that has been and will be shed in this struggle of the oppressed against the oppressor? Shall you tell me this, and must I be so very as slave as not to repel it?

Lord Norbury— *"A different conduct would have better become one who had endeavoured to overthrow the laws and liberties of his country"*.

I who fear not to approach the Omnipotent Judge to answer for the conduct of my whole life, am I to be appalled and falsified by a mere remnant of mortality here? By you, too, who if it were possible to collect all the innocent blood that you have shed in your unhallowed ministry in one great reservoir, your lordship might swim in it.

Lord Norbury—*"I exhort you not to depart this life with such sentiments of rooted hostility to your country as those which you have expressed'*.

Let no man dare, when I am dead, to charge me with dishonour; let no man attaint my memory by believing that I could have engaged in any cause but that of my country's liberty and independence; or that I could have become the pliant minion of power in the oppression and misery of my countrymen. The proclamation of the Provisional Government speaks for my views; no inference can be tortured from it to countenance barbarity or debasement at home, or subjection, humiliation, or treachery from abroad. I would not have submitted to a foreign oppressor, for the same reason that I would resist the domestic tyrant. In the dignity of freedom, I would have fought upon the threshold of my country, and its enemy should only enter by passing over my lifeless corpse. And am I, who lived but for my country, who have subjected myself to the dangers of the jealous and watchful oppressor, and now to the bondage of the grave, only to give my countrymen their rights, and my country her independence—am I to be loaded with calumny and not suffered to resent it? No, God forbid!

Here Lord Norbury told Emmet that his sentiments and language disgraced his family and his education, but more particularly his father, Dr. Emmet, who was a man, if alive, that would not countenance such opinions. To which Emmet replied:—

If the spirits of the illustrious dead participate in the concerns and cares of those who were dear to them in this transitory life, O! ever dear and venerated shade of my departed father, look down with scrutiny upon the conduct of your suffering son, and see if I have, even for a moment, deviated from those principles of morality and patriotism which it was your care to instil into my youthful mind, and for which I am now about to offer up my life. My lords, you seem impatient for the sacrifice. The blood for which you thirst is not congealed by the artificial terrors which surround your victim [the soldiery filled and surrounded the Sessions House]—it circulates warmly and unruffled through the channels which God created for noble purposes, but which you are now bent to destroy, for purposes so grievous that they cry to heaven. Be yet patient! I have but a few words more to say. I am going to my cold and silent grave; my lamp of life is nearly extinguished; my race is run; the grave opens to receive me, and I sink into its bosom.

I have but one request to ask at my departure from this world; it is—THE CHARITY OF ITS SILENCE. Let no man write my epitaph; for as no man who knows my motives dare now vindicate them, let not prejudice or ignorance asperse them. Let them and me rest in obscurity and peace, and my name remain uninscribed, until other times and other men can do justice to my character. When my country takes her place among the nations of the earth, then, and not till then, let my epitaph be written. I have done.

The Young Irelanders

The failure of the 1798 Rebellion led to renewed nationalist efforts into peaceful political organising, most successfully in the form of The Liberator, Daniel O'Connell. O'Connell successfully mobilised Catholic Ireland and secured Catholic emancipation in 1829. O'Connell's reformist approach was too moderate for some, and radical nationalist splinters emerged. One of these was Young Ireland, or Éire Óg, formed around a group of young radicals breaking away from O'Connell's Repeal Association, which campaigned for the repeal of the Act of Union that merged Ireland with Britain. These men were initially grouped around the nationalist weekly newspaper *The Nation*.

Thomas Davis, one of the co-founders of *The Nation*, was considered the intellectual heart of the movement. A poet, journalist, and lawyer, Davis channelled his talents into fostering a sense of Irish nationhood and cultural pride. Inspired by the currents of romantic nationalism from the continent, Davis saw the purpose of *The Nation* as being to promote a strong sense of Irish cultural unity – including encouraging use of the Irish language, something O'Connell never concerned himself with. Davis's poetry, including now iconic works like *"A Nation Once Again,"* became anthems of national awakening. That song has become one of the most popular examples of Irish rebel music, its popularity enduring to this day.

John Mitchel brought a fiercer edge to the Young Irelanders. A solicitor by training, Mitchel joined *The Nation* after Davis's death at age 30. He quickly gained notoriety for his militancy. Where Davis sought unity through culture, Mitchel's focus was on encouraging direct confrontation with British oppression. His fiery prose condemned British policies, particularly during the Great Famine (1845–1852), which he blamed on deliberate neglect rather than natural disaster. In 1848, he founded his own newspaper, *The United Irishman*, where he openly called for armed rebellion against British rule. This radical stance led to his arrest and transport to the prison colony of Van Diemen's Land – modern day Tasmania. The ever-resilient Mitchel managed to escape to America. There, he continued to write passionately for Ireland's freedom, establishing a new venture called *The Irish Citizen*. Always a man of the right and opposed to any kind of egalitarian thinking, while in America Mitchel embraced the Confederate struggle as analogous to Ireland's and even defended chattel slavery on racial grounds. In 1875, Mitchel won a seat in parliament on his return to Ireland, but the House of Commons declared his election ineligible due to his status as a felon. He died the same year.

James Fintan Lalor emerged as a powerful and popular voice of Ireland's struggle with a series of letters to *The Nation*. Writing indignantly during The Great Famine, like Mitchel he blamed British land policies for the catastrophe. Thus, land reform and economic justice became the central themes of Lalor's advocacy and his vision for Irish sovereignty, "The soil of Ireland for the people of Ireland" became his rallying cry – a demand that resonated with a peasantry ground down by evictions and rack-rents. Lalor's focus on the land question and the economic aspect of Ireland's subjugation would prove very influential on future nationalist leaders, most notably Pádraig Pearse, James Connolly and Arthur Griffith. Lalor's ideas found a fiercer outlet in *The Irish Felon*, a short-lived radical paper he co-edited in 1848. Here, he began to advocate for a broader uprising in the form of armed rebellions, and used the paper to promote The Felon Club, a revolutionary militia. That year, he joined the Young Irelanders' ill-fated rebellion — a chaotic affair based out of County Tipperary, that collapsed under famine-weakened support and British suppression. Arrested and briefly imprisoned, Lalor's fragile health deteriorated, but his resolve never wavered up to his death in 1849 at the age of 42.

A Nation Once Again

Thomas Davis

I.

When boyhood's fire was in my blood
I read of ancient freemen
For Greece and Rome who bravely stood,
Three Hundred Men and Three Men.
And then I prayed I yet might see
Our fetters rent in twain,
And Ireland, long a province, be
A Nation once again.

II.

And, from that time, through wildest woe,
That hope has shone, a far light;
Nor could love's brightest summer glow
Outshine that solemn starlight:
It seemed to watch above my head
In forum, field and fane;
Its angel voice sang round my bed,
"A Nation once again."

III.

It whispered, too, that "freedom's ark
And service high and holy,
Would be profaned by feelings dark
And passions vain or lowly:
For freedom comes from God's right hand,
And needs a godly train;
And righteous men must make our land
A Nation once again."

IV.

So, as I grew from boy to man,
I bent me to that bidding—
My spirit of each selfish plan
And cruel passion ridding;
For, thus I hoped some day to aid—
Oh! can *such* hope be vain?—
When my dear country shall be made
A Nation once again

A Second Year's Work

Thomas Davis

It was a bold experiment to establish *The Nation*. Our success is more honourable to Ireland than to us, for it was by defying evil customs and bad prejudices we succeeded.

Let us prove this.

Religion has for ages been so mixed with Irish quarrels that it is often hard to say whether patriotism or superstition was the animating principle of an Irish leader, and whether political rapacity or bigoted zeal against bigotry was the motive of an oppressor. Yet in no country was this more misplaced in our day than in Ireland. Our upper classes were mostly Episcopalians—masters not merely of the institutions, but the education and moral force of the country. The middle ranks and much of the peasantry of one of our greatest provinces were Presbyterians, obstinate in their simple creed— proud of their victories, yet apprehensive of oppression. The rest of the population were Catholics, remarkable for piety and tenderness, but equally noted for ignorance and want of self-reliance. To mingle politics and religion in such a country was to blind men to their common secular interests, to render political union impossible, and national independence hopeless.

We grappled with the difficulty. We left sacred things to consecrated hands—theology and discipline to Churchmen. We preached a nationality that asked after no man's creed (*friend's or foe's*); and now, after our Second Year's Work, we have got a *practical* as well as a verbal admission that religion is a thing between man and God—that no citizen is to be hooted, or abused, or marked down because he holds any imaginable creed, or changes it any conceivable number of times.

We are proudly conscious that, in preaching these great truths with success, we have done more to convince the Protestants that they may combine with the Catholics and get from under the shield of England than if we had proved that the Repeal of the Union would double the ears of their corn fields.

There had been a long habit of looking to foreign arms or English mercy for redress. We have shared the labours of O'Connell and O'Brien in impressing on the People that self-reliance is the only liberator. We have, not in vain, taught that, though the concessions of England or the sympathy of others was to be welcomed and used, still they would be best won by dignity and strength; and that, whether they came or not, Ireland could redress herself by patience, energy, and resolution.

Yet, deficient as the People were in genuine self-reliance, they had been pampered into the belief that they were highly educated, nobly represented, successful in every science and art, and that consequently their misery was a mysterious fate, for which there was no remedy in human means. We believe we have convinced them of the contrary of this. Ireland has done great things. She has created an unrivalled music and oratory, taken a first place in lyric poetry, displayed great valour, ready wit—has been a pattern of domestic virtue and faith under persecution; and lately has again advanced herself and her fame by deliberate temperance, by organised abstinence from crime, and by increasing political discipline. Yet there is that worst of all facts on the face of the census, that most of the Irish can neither read nor write; there is evidence in every exhibition that this land, which produced Barry, Forde, Maclise, and Burton, is ignorant of the fine arts; and proof in every shop or factory of the truth of Kane's motto, that industrial ignorance is a prime obstacle to our wealth. We have no national theatre, either in books or performance; and though we have got of late some classes of prose literature—national fiction, for instance—we have yet to write our history, our statistics, and much of our science.

We have week after week candidly told these things to the People, and, instead of quarrelling with us, or running off to men who said "the Irish have succeeded in everything," they hearkened to us, and raised our paper into a circulation beyond most of the leaders of the London press, and immensely beyond any other journal that ever was in Ireland. What is more cheering still, they have set about curing their defects. They are founding Repeal Reading-rooms. They have noted down their ignorance in many portions of agriculture, manufactures, commerce, history, literature, and fine arts; and they are working with the Agricultural Societies, forming Polytechnic Institutions for the improvement of manufactures, and giving and demanding support to the antiquarian and historical and artistical books and institutions in Ireland. Large *classes* wished well to, and small ones supported each of these projects before; but in this journal *all* classes were canvassed incessantly, and not in vain—and if there be unanimity now, we claim some credit for ourselves, but much more for the People, who did not resent harsh truth, and took advice that affronted their vanity.

A political impatience and intolerance have too often been seen in this country. It is one of the vices of slaves to use free speech to insult all who do not praise their faults and their friends and their caprices. We rejoice, in looking over our files, to see how rarely we were personal and how generally we recognised the virtues of political foes. It is an equal pleasure to recall that in many questions, but especially in reference to the Liberal Members not in the Association, we stood between an impolitic fury and its destined victims. The People bore with us, and then agreed with us. We told them that men able and virtuous—men who had gone into Parliament when Repeal was a Whig buggaboo to frighten the Tories, were not to be hallooed from their seats because Repeal had suddenly grown into a national demand. These men, we said, may become your allies, if you do not put them upon their mettle by your rudeness and impatience. If they join you, they will be faster and more useful friends than men who compensate for every defect by pledge-bolting at command.

Mr. O'Connell, who had at first seemed to incline to the opposite opinion, concurred with us. Mr. O'Brien was zealous on the same side; the "premature pledges" were postponed to their fit time—an election—and the people induced to apply themselves to the Registries, as the true means of getting Repeal members.

We have maintained and advanced our foreign policy—the recognition and study of other countries beside England, and a careful separation of ourselves from England's crimes. We have, we believe, not neglected those literary, antiquarian, and historical teachings, and those popular projects which we pointed to last year as part of our labours; and we are told that the poetry of *The Nation* has not been worse than in our first year. But these things are more personal, less indicative of national progress, and therefore less interesting than our success in producing political tolerance, increased efforts for education, and that final concession to religious liberty—the right to change without even verbal persecution.

The last year has been a year of hard work and hard trial to the country and to us. Our first year was spent in rousing and animating—the second in maintaining, guiding, and restraining. Its motto is, "Bide your time." Never had a People more temptation to be rash; and it is our proudest feeling that in our way we aided the infinitely greater powers of O'Connell till his imprisonment, and of O'Brien thereafter, to keep in the passion, while they kept up the spirit of the People.

They and we succeeded.

The People saw the darling of their hearts dragged to trial, yet they never rioted; they found month after month go by in the disgusting details of a trial at bar, yet, instead of desponding, they improved their organisation, studied their history and statistics—increased in dignity, modesty, and strength. At length came the imprisonment; we almost doubted them, but they behaved gloriously—they recognised their wrongs, but they crossed their arms—they were neither terrified, disordered, nor divided—they promptly obeyed their new leaders, and, with shut teeth, swore that their "only vengeance should be victory." They succeeded—bore their triumph as well as their defeat, and are now taking breath for a fresh effort at education, organisation, and conciliation.

It is something to have laboured through a Second Year for such a People. Let them go on as they have begun—growing more thoughtful, more temperate, more educated, more resolute—let them complete their parish organisation, carry out their registries, and, above all, establish those Reading-rooms which will inform and strengthen them into liberty; and, ere many years' work, the Green Flag will be saluted by Europe, and Ireland will be a Nation. The

People have shown that their spirit, their discipline, and their modesty can be relied on; they have but to exhibit that greatest virtue which their enemies deny them—perseverance—and all will be well.

No Redress – No Enquiry

Thomas Davis

The British Parliament has refused to redress our wrongs, or even to inquire into them. For five long nights were they compelled to listen to arguments, facts, and principles proving that we were sorely oppressed. They did not deny the facts— they did not refute the reasoning—they did not undermine the principles—but they would not try to right us.

"We inherit the right of hatred for six centuries of oppression; what will you do to prove your repentance, and propitiate our revenge?"—and the answer is, "That's an old story, we wish to hear no more of it."

Legislature of Britain, you shall hear more of it!

The growing race of Irishmen are the first generation of freemen which Ireland nursed these three centuries. The national schools may teach them only the dry elements of knowledge adulterated with Anglicism, and Trinity College may teach them bigotry, along with graceful lore and strong science; but there are other schools at work. There is a national art, and there is an Irish literature growing up.

Day after day the choice of the young men discover that genius needs a country to honour and be loved by. The Irish Press is beginning to teach the People to know themselves and their history; to know other nations, and to feel the rights and duties of citizens. The agitation, whose surges sweep through every nook of the island, converts all that the People learn to national uses; nothing is lost, nothing is adverse; neutrality is help, and all power is converted into power for Ireland.

Ireland is changing the loose tradition of her wrongs into history and ballad; and though justice, repentance, or retribution may make her cease to need vengeance, she will immortally remember her bondage, her struggles, her glories, and her disasters. Till her suffering ceases that remembrance will rouse her passions and nerve her arm. May she not forgive till she is no longer oppressed; and when she forgives, may she never forget!

Why need we repeat the tale of present wretchedness? Seven millions and a half of us are Presbyterians and Catholics, and our whole ecclesiastical funds go to the gorgeous support of the Clergy of the remaining 800,000, who are Episcopalians. Where else on *earth* does a similar injury and dishonour exist? Nowhere; 'twas confessed it existed nowhere. Would it weaken the empire to abolish this? Confessedly not, but would give it some chance of holding together. Would it injure Protestantism? You say not. Idle wealth is fatal to a Church, and supremacy bears out every proud and generous convert. Why is it maintained? The answer is directly given—"England (that is, the English aristocracy) is bigoted," and no Ministry dare give you redress. These are the very words of Captain Rous, the Tory member for Westminster, and the whole House assented to the fact. If you cannot redress—if you will not go into inquiry, lest this redress, so needed by us, should be fatal to your selfish power, then loose your hold of us, and we will redress ourselves; and we will do so with less injury to any class than you possibly could, for a free nation may be generous—a struggling one will not and ought not to be so.

We are most dishonestly taxed for *your* debts; the fact was not denied—an ominous silence declared that not a halfpenny of that mighty mortgage would be taken off our shoulders.

You raise five millions a year from us, and you spend it on English commissioners, English dockyards, English museums, English ambition, and English pleasures. With an enormous taxation, our public offices have been removed to London, and you threaten to remove our Courts of Justice, and our Lord Lieutenancy, the poor trapping of old nationhood. We have no arsenals, no public employment here; our literary, scientific, and charitable institutions, so bountifully endowed by a Native Legislature, you have forced away, till, out of that enormous surplus revenue raised here, not £10,000 a year comes back for such purposes, while you have heaped hundred upon hundred thousand into the lap of every English institution. For National Education you dribble out £50,000 a year— not enough for our smallest province. Will you redress these things? No, but you boast of your liberality in giving us anything.

"Oh, but you are not overtaxed," says Peel; "see, your Post-office produces nothing to the revenue." Ay, Sir, our Post-office, which levies the same rates as the English Post-office, produces nothing; Ireland is too poor to make even a penny-postage pay its own cost. No stronger mark of a stagnant trade could be adduced. "And then we lowered your spirit duty." Yes you did, because it brought in less than the lower duty. What single tax did you take off, except when it had been raised so high, or the country had declined so low, that it ceased to be productive? You increased our taxation up to the end of the war two and a half times more rapidly than you did your own, and you diminished our taxation after the war thirty times less rapidly.

You have a fleet of steamers now—you had none in 1817, says some pattern of English Senators, whose constituents are bound to subscribe a few school-books for him if they mean to continue him as their delegate.

And my Lord Eliot says our exports and imports have increased. We wish your Lordship would have separate accounts kept that we might know how much. But they *have* increased—ay, they have; and they are provisions. And our population has increased: and when we had one-half the number of People to feed we sent out a tenth of the provisions we send away now. This is ruin, not prosperity. We had weavers, iron-workers, glass-makers, and fifty other flourishing trades. They sold their goods to Irishmen in exchange for beef and mutton, and bread, and bacon, and potatoes. The Irish provisions were not exported—they were eaten in Ireland. They are exported now—for Irish artisans, without work, must live on the refuse of the soil, and Irish peasants must eat lumpers or starve. Part of the exports go to buy rags and farming tools, which once went for clothes and all other goods to Irish operatives, and the rest goes to raise money to pay absentee rents and imperial taxes. Will you tax our absentees? Will you employ our artisans? Will you abate your taxes, or spend them among us? No; you refuse redress—you refuse inquiry.

Your conquests and confiscations have given us land tenures alien to the country and deadly to the peasant. Will you interfere in property to save him, as you interfered to oppress him? You hint that you might inquire, but you only offered redress in an Arms' Bill—to prostrate the poor man, to violate the sanctity of his home, to brand him, and leave him at the mercy of his local tyrant.

Will you equalise the franchise, and admit us, in proportion to our numbers, into your Senate, and let us try there for redress? You may inquire, perhaps, some other time; if much pressed, you may consider some increase of the franchise—you decline to open the representation.

And if England will do none of these things, will she allow us, for good or ill, to govern ourselves, and see if we cannot redress our own griefs? "No, never, never," she says, "though all Ireland cried for it—never! Her fields shall be manured with the shattered limbs of her sons, and her hearths quenched in their blood; but never, while England has a ship or a soldier, shall Ireland be free."

And this is your answer? We shall see—we shall see!

And now, Englishmen, listen to us! Though you were to-morrow to give us the best tenures on earth—though you were to equalise Presbyterian, Catholic, and Episcopalian—though you were to give us the amplest representation in your Senate—though you were to restore our absentees, disencumber us of your debt, and redress every one of our fiscal wrongs—and though, in addition to all this, you plundered the treasuries of the world to lay gold at our feet, and exhausted the resources of your genius to do us worship and honour—still we tell you—we tell you, in the names of liberty and country—we tell you, in the name of enthusiastic hearts, thoughtful souls, and fearless spirits—we tell you, by the past, the present and the future, we would spurn your gifts, if the condition were that Ireland should remain a province. We tell you, and all whom it may concern, come what may—bribery or deceit, justice, policy, or war—we tell you, in the name of Ireland, that Ireland shall be a Nation!

Address to the College historical society

Thomas Davis

The following is the conclusion of a famous speech by Davis delivered to the College Historical Society in Trinity College Dublin.

To each age has God given a career of possible improvement; it may exceed, it may fall short of that in other ages. The march during the daylight of our age may he limited by the time and training; but we have it in our power to accelerate that march.

The time is past when the omnipotence of the sword might excuse the sentimental, or learned, or melancholy retirement. The man who now avoids his citizenship has no defence but imbecility; for if we have sagacity and learning he has power and sins in folding up his talent want of zeal to use it. He lacks not means, but a virtuous will.

I would especially desire the diffusion of civic zeal, because in it I see the means, the only means, of human improvement. The effect of modern civilisation up to a certain point has been good; it has tended to free man from the dominion of an armed minority, who stupefied and worked the human race as if they were so many machines which they had made, and could make, and had no reason to abstain from abusing, save the prudence of perpetuating them. This step has been taken in some countries, and seems likely to be taken in all. But on the shore of democracy is a monstrous danger; no phantasm is it, but alas! too real-the violence and forwardness of selfish men, regardful only of physical comfort, ready to sacrifice to it all sentiments – the generous, the pious, the just (victims in their order), till general corruption, anarchy, despotism, and moral darkness shall re-barbarise the earth. A great man has said, if you would qualify Democracy for power, you must "purify their morals, and warm their faith, if that be possible." How awful a doubt! But it is not the morality of laws, nor the religion of sects, that will do this. It is the habit of rejoicing in high aspirations and holy emotions; it is charity in thought, word, and act; it is generous faith, and the practice of self-sacrificing virtue.

To educate the heart and strengthen the intellect of man are the means of ennobling him. To strain every nerve to this end is the duty from which no one aware of it can shrink. A sphere of influence belongs to every man and every age, and over every man, and every nation, and every succeeding age; but that of action is more confined. The influence of moral power extends but gradually and indirectly over contemporary foreign nations. Those whose acts can directly influence the republic of nations are few, and at so lonely an elevation above common habits that they usually lose our common sympathies, and their power is a curse. But no man is without a sufficient sphere of action, and of direct influence. I speak now of private life; in it, blessed be God! our people are tender, generous, and true-hearted. BUT, GENTILMEN, YOU HAVE A COUNTRY. The people among whom we were born, with whom we live, for whom, if our minds are in health, we have most sympathy, ore those over whom we have power – power to make them wise, great, good. Reason points out our native land as the field for our exertions, and tells us that without patriotism a profession of benevolence is the cloak of the selfish man; and does not sentiment confirm the decree of reason? The country of our birth, our education, of our recollections, ancestral, personal, national; the country of our loves, our friendships, our-hopes; our country – : the cosmopolite is unnatural, base – I would fain say, impossible. To act on a world is for those above it, not of it. Patriotism is human philanthropy.

Gentlemen, many of you possess, more of you are growing into the possession of, great powers – powers which were given you for good, which you may use for evil. I trust that not as adventurers, or rash meddlers, will you enter on public life. But to enter on it in some way or other the state of mind in Ireland will compel you. You must act as citizens, and it is well, "non nobis solum nati sumus, ortusque nostri partem patria vindicat." Patriotism once felt to be a duty becomes so. To act in politics is a matter of duty everywhere; here, of necessity. To make that action honourable to yourselves, and serviceable to your country, is a matter of choice. In your public career you will be solicited by a thousand temptations to sully your souls with the gold and place of a foreign court, or the transient breath of a dishonest popularity; dishonest, when adverse to the good, though flattering to the prejudices of the people.

You now abound in patriotism, and are sceptical of public corruption; yet most assuredly, if you be eloquent and strong-thinking, threats and bribes will be held out to you. You will be solicited to become the barking misleaders of a faction, or the gazehounds of a minister – dogs who can tell a patriot afar off. Be jealous of your honour and your virtue then; yield not. Bid back the tempter. Do not grasp remorse. Nay, if it be not a vain thought, in such hours of mortal doubt, when the tempted spirit rocks to and fro, pause and recall one of your youthful evenings, and remember the warning voice of your old companion, who felt as a friend, and used a friend's liberty.

Let the voice of his warning rise upon your ear, think he stands before you as he does now, telling you in such moments, when pride or luxury or wrath make you Waver, to return to communings with nature's priests, the Burns, the Wordsworths, the Shakespeares, but, above all, to nature's self. She waits with a mother's longings for the wanderer; fling yourselves into her arms, and as your heart beats upon her bosom your native nobility will return, and thoughts divine as the divinest you ever felt will bear you unscathed through the furnace. Pardon the presumption, pardon the hope ('tis one of my dearest now), "forsan et haec olim meminisse juvabit." And I do not fear that any of you will be found among Ireland's foes. To her every energy should be consecrated. Were she prosperous she would have man to serve her, though their hearts were cold in her cause. But it is because her people lieth down in misery and riseth to suffer, it is therefore you should be more deeply devoted.

Your country will, I fear, need all your devotion. She has no foreign friend. Beyond the limits of green Erin there is none to aid her. She may gain by the feuds of the stranger; she cannot hope for his peaceful help, be he distant, be he near; her trust is in her sons. You are Irish-men. She relies on your devotion. She solicits it by her present distraction and misery. No! her past distraction – her present woe. We have no more war bills: we have a mendicant bill for Ireland. The poor and the pest-houses are full, yet the valleys of her country and the streets of her metropolis swarm with the starving. Her poet has described her:

"More dear in her sorrow, her gloom, and her showers, Than the rest of the world in its sunniest hours."

And if she be miserable, if "homely age hath the alluring beauty took from her poor cheek, then who hath wasted it?" The stranger from without, by means of the traitor within. Perchance 'tis a fanciful thing, yet in the misfortunes of Ireland, in her laurelled martyrs, in those who died "persecuted men for a persecuted country," in the necessity she was under of bearing the palms to deck her best to the scaffold-foot and the lost battlefield, she has seemed to me chastened for some great future.

I have thought I saw her spirit from her dwelling, her sorrowing place among the tombs, rising, not without melancholy, yet with a purity and brightness beyond other nations, and I thought that God had made her purpose firm and her heart just; and I knew that if He had, small though she were, His angels would have charge over her, "lest at any time she should dash her foot against a stone." And I have prayed that I might live to see the day when, amid the reverence of those once her foes, her sons would:

"Like the leaves of the Shamrock unite,
A partition of sects from one foot stalk of right;
Give each his full share of the earth and the sky
Nor fatten the slave where the serpent would die."

But not only by her sufferings does Ireland call upon you. Her past history, furnishes something to awake proud recollections. I speak not of that remote and mysterious time when the men of Tyre traded to her well-known shores, and every art of peace und a home on her soil; and her armies, not unused to conquest, traversed Britain and Gaul. Nor yet of that time when her colleges offered a hospitable asylum to the learned and the learning of every land, and her missions bore knowledge and piety through savage Europe; nor yet of her gallant and romantic struggles, against the Dane, and Saxon, and Norman; still less of her hardy wars, in which her interest was sacrificed to a too-devoted loyalty, in many a successful, many a disastrous battle. Not of these. I speak of sixty years ago. The memory is fresh, the example pure, the success inspiring. I SPEAK OF "THE LIFETIME OF IRELAND" (Ireland was then a confederation of local governments, and her stubborn and protracted resistance may be added to the many such incidences accumulated by Sismondi to show the greater stability and greater defensive forces of countries with a minute local organisation and self-government over the larger centralised powers.)

But if neither the present nor the past can rouse you, let the sun of hope, the beams of the future, awake you to exertion in the cause of patriotism. Seek, oh seek to make your country not behind at least in the progress of the nations. Education, the apostle of progress, hath gone forth. Knowledge is not virtue, but may be rendered its precursor. Virtue is not alone enjoyment, is not all happiness; but be sure, when the annunciation of virtue comes, the advent of happiness is at hand. Seek to take your country forward in her progress to that goal, where she, in common with the other nations, may hear that annunciation of virtue, and share that advent of happiness, holiness, and peace.

Gentlemen, I have done. You have been disappointed; you expected, your partiality expected, from me prescriptions to make the best of good speeches, at the bar, pulpit, and senate-all in a brilliant address. Yet, though to hear them has given you little pleasure, and to write them has cost me little time, the thoughts are not rash or inconsiderate; they were the best I had. It would have been easier, much easier, for me to have written rhetorical precepts, and the distinctions of a shallow metaphysics, and to have conveyed such thoughts in a showy diction and with pointed periods. I should have avoided the trouble of combining my scattered thoughts on the subject of our education, but I should have violated my conscious duty. I should have won a louder and more frequent cheer. You would have cheered and have forgotten me. I shall heartily wish you, gentlemen, what each of you will, I know, wish me in return: that you may struggle and succeed in a career, honourable and useful to yourselves and those who are dear to you, in time; and which, I say it in the sincerest solemnity of my heart, may render you better fitted for eternity.

The Library of Ireland

Thomas Davis

While the Gaelic-speaking people of Ireland were restricted to traditional legends, songs, and histories, a library was provided for those who used English by the genius and industry of men whose names have vanished—a fate common to them with the builder of the Pyramids, the inventor of letters, and other benefactors of mankind. Moore has given, in *Captain Rock*, an imperfect catalogue of this library. The scientific course seems to have been rather limited, as Ovid's *Art of* (let us rather say essay on) *Love* was the only abstract work; but it contained biographies of *Captain Freney the Robber*, and of *Redmond O'Hanlon the Rapparee*—wherein, we fear, O'Hanlon was made, by a partial pen, rather more like Freney than history warrants; dramas such as the *Battle of Aughrim*, written apparently by some Alsatian Williamite; lyrics of love, unhoused save by the watch; imperial works, too, as *Moll Flanders*; and European literature—*Don Beliants, and the Seven Champions*. Whether they were imported, or originally produced for the grooms of the dissolute gentry, may be discussed; but it seems certain that their benign influence spread, on one side, to the farmers' and shopkeepers' sons, and, on the other, to the cadets of the great families—and were, in short, the classics of tipsy Ireland. The deadly progress of temperance, politics, and democracy has sent them below their original market, and in ten years the collector will pay a guinea apiece for them.

During the Emancipation struggle this indecent trash shrunk up, and a totally different literature circulated. The Orange party regaled themselves chiefly with theology, but the rest of the country (still excepting the classes sheltered by their Gaelic tongue) formed a literature more human, and quite as serious. There occasionally is great vigour in the biographies of Lord Edward, Robert Emmet, and other popular heroes chronicled at that time; but the long interview of Emmet with Sarah Curran, the night before his execution, is a fair specimen of the accuracy of these works. The songs were intense enough, occasionally controversial, commonly polemical, always extravagant; the Granu Wails and Shan-Van-Vochts of the Catholic agitation cannot be too soon obsolete. The famous Waterford song:—

"O'Connell's come to town,
And he'll put the Orange down,
And by the heavenly G—— he'll wear the crown,
Says the Shan Van Vocht!"

is characteristic of the zeal, discretion, and style of these once powerful lyrics. A history of the authorship of these biographies and songs would be interesting, and is perhaps still possible. The reprint in the series of Hugh O'Reilly's Irish history—albeit, a mass of popular untruth was put at the end of it—shows as if some more considerate mind had begun to influence these publications. They, too, are fast vanishing, and will yet be sought to illustrate their times.

In the first class we have described there was nothing to redeem their stupid indecency and ruffianism; in the latter, however one may grieve at their bigotry, and dislike their atrocious style, there were purity, warmth, and a high purpose.

The "Useful Knowledge Society" period arrived in Britain, and flooded that island with cheap tracts on algebra and geometry, chemistry, theology, and physiology. Penny Magazines told every man how his stockings were wove, how many drunkards were taken up per hour in Southwark, how the geese were plucked from which the author got his pens, how many pounds weight of lead (with the analysis thereof, and an account of the Cornish mines by way of parenthesis) were in the types for each page, and the nature of the rags (so many per cent. beggars, so many authors, so many shoe-boys) from which the paper of the all-important, man and money-saving Penny Magazine was made. On its being suggested that man was more than a statistician, or a dabbler in mathematics, a *moral* series (warranted Benthamite) was issued to teach people how they should converse at meals—how to choose their wives, masters, and servants by phrenological developments, and how to live happily, like "Mr. Hard-and-Comfortable," the Yellow Quaker.

Unluckily for us, there was no great popular passion in Ireland at the time, and our communication with England had been greatly increased by steamers and railways, by the Whig alliance, by democratic sympathy, and by the transference of our political capital to Westminster. Tracts, periodicals, and the whole horde of Benthamy rushed in. Without manufactures, without trade, without comfort to palliate such degradation, we were proclaimed converts to Utilitarianism. The Irish press thought itself imperial, because it reflected that of London—Nationality was called a vulgar superstition, and a general European Trades' Union, to be followed by a universal Republic, became the final aspirations of "all enlightened men." At the same time the National Schools were spreading the elements of science and the means of study through the poorer classes, and their books were merely intellectual.

Between all these influences Ireland promised to become a farm for Lancashire, with the wisdom and moral rank of that district, without its wealth, when there came a deliverer—the Repeal agitation.

Its strain gradually broke the Whig alliance and the Chartist sympathy. Westminster ceased to be the city towards which the Irish bowed and made pilgrimage. An organisation, centring in Dublin, connected the People; and an oratory full of Gaelic passion and popular idiom galvanised them. Thus there has been, from 1842—when the Repeal agitation became serious—an incessant progress in Literature and Nationality. A Press, Irish in subjects, style, and purpose, has been formed—a National Poetry has grown up—the National Schools have prepared their students for the more earnest study of National politics and history—the classes most hostile to the agitation are converts to its passions; and when Lord Heytesbury recently expressed his wonder at finding "Irish prejudices" in the most cultivated body in Ireland, he only bore witness to an aristocratic Nationality of which he could have found countless proofs beside.

Yet the power of British utilitarian literature continues. The wealthy classes are slowly getting an admirable and a costly National Literature from Petrie, and O'Donovan, and Ferguson, and Lefanu, and the *University Magazine*. The poorer are left to the newspaper and the meeting, and an occasional serial of very moderate merits. That class, now becoming the rulers of Ireland, who have taste for the higher studies, but whose means are small, have only a few scattered works within their reach, and some of them, not content to use these exclusively, are driven to foreign studies and exposed to alien influence.

To give to the country a National Library, exact enough for the wisest, high enough for the purest, and cheap enough for all readers, appears the object of "The Library of Ireland."

Look at the subjects—*A History of the Volunteers*, Memoirs of Hugh O'Neill, of Tone, of Owen Roe, of Grattan, Collections of Irish Ballads and Songs, and so forth. It would take one a month, with the use of all the libraries of Dublin, to get the history of the Volunteers. In Wilson's so-called history you will get a number of addresses and 300 pages of irrelevant declamation for eight or ten shillings. Try further, and you must penetrate through the manuscript catalogues of Trinity College and the Queen's Inns (the last a wilderness) to find the pamphlets and newspapers containing what you want; yet the history of the Volunteers is one interesting to every class, and equally popular in every province.

Hugh O'Neill—he found himself an English tributary, his clan beaten, his country despairing. He organised his clan into an army, defeated by arms and policy the best generals and statesmen of Elizabeth, and gave Ireland a pride and a hope which never deserted her since. Yet the only written history of him lies in an Irish MS. in the Vatican, unprinted, untranslated, uncopied; and the Irishman who would know his life must grope through Moryson, and Ware, and O'Sullivan in unwilling libraries, and in books whose price would support a student for two winters.

Of Tone and Grattan—the wisest and most sublime of our last generation—there are lives, and valuable ones; but such as the rich only will buy, and the leisurely find time to read.

The rebellion of 1641—a mystery and a lie—is it not time to let every man look it in the face? The Irish Brigade—a marvellous reality to few, a proud phantom to most of us—shall we not all, rich and poor, learn in good truth how the Berserk Irish bore up in the winter streets of Cremona, or the gorgeous Brigade followed Clare's flashing plumes right through the great column of Fontenoy?

Irish Ballads and Songs—why (except that *Spirit of the Nation* which we so audaciously put together), the popular ballads and songs are the faded finery of the West End, the foul parodies of St. Giles's, the drunken rigmarole of the black Helots—or, as they are touchingly classed in the streets, "sentimental, comic, and nigger songs." Yet Banim, and Griffin, and Furlong, Lover and Ferguson, Drennan and Callanan, have written ballads and songs as true to Ireland as ever MacNeill's or Conyngham's were to Scotland; and firmly do we hope to see with every second lad in Ireland a volume of honest, noble, Irish ballads, as well thumbed as a Lowland Burns or a French Beranger, and sweetly shall yet come to us from every milking-field and harvest-home songs not too proudly joined to the sweetest music in the world.

This country of ours is no sand bank, thrown up by some recent caprice of earth. It is an ancient land, honoured in the archives of civilisation, traceable into antiquity by its piety, its valour, and its sufferings. Every great European race has sent its stream to the river of Irish mind. Long wars, vast organisations, subtle codes, beacon crimes, leading virtues, and self-mighty men were here. If we live influenced by wind and sun and tree, and not by the passions and deeds of the past, we are a thriftless and a hopeless People.

enslish Rule

John Mitchel

The Nation, 7 March, 1846.

I s England henceforth to rule Ireland by the laws or by the bayonet? This is a question which will soon press for an answer; and we only anticipate events in answering it here, and now – *By neither.*

Ireland hates English law, is disaffected towards English government, suspects, abhors the legislature which enacts those laws, the officers who administer them, and the military garrison which alone maintains them. Every day makes this breach wider – it will not close, *and it ought not.*

Then comes the other, the *last* alternative – the bayonet; and undoubtedly by a strong military occupation and stringent insurrection acts, a kind of *quasi* government may be carried on here for a time, provided a sufficient number of troops can be spared from the Eastern wars now raging, and the Western wars that threaten to break out. Gaols and halters, artillery and hangmen, may "pacificate" for a little while – yet is the end coming.

There is a newspaper published in London called the *Examiner*, one of their "Liberal" papers (to use a word by which one of the

English factions designates itself). The number of that paper published on Saturday last contains an article remonstrating with their Government against the new Coercion Bill which it has proposed; and, after showing the hardship of transporting a farmer for overstaying sunset at his market, or for taking refuge in a public-house at nightfall lest he be found straying, this English journalist thus continues: –

"Can any one suppose a mode of rendering *English rule* more obnoxious, not merely to the lower, but to the middle class of Irish?"

The humane intercessor of the *Examiner* is plainly unconscious of the cool insolence of this language. The man means well: he says to his Government, "Let us not trample these poor devils of Irish altogether down into the earth – let our yoke be somewhat easier, our burden only a little lighter upon them – let us not break utterly the bruised reed – 'tis cruel, unmanly – all the world will cry shame upon us." His idea is one of contemptuous compassion: his reasoning is the preamble of "Martin's Act" – whereas it is expedient that the inferior animals should not be wantonly tortured.

We desire to know whether it is tolerable that we should remain subject to a country in which our very friends and advocates can use an argument like this. Even while they plead for us, they quietly take for granted the impossibility of a union upon equal terms between the two countries – coolly assume that the one is, and must remain, *under* the other – that the problem to be solved is not how Ireland is to be made a partaker in what they call their "British Constitution," but how "English rule" is to be made endurable to her.

This very unconsciousness of the enormity involved in such an assumption, makes it the more enormous. If we found it in the columns of the *Times*, or *Chronicle*, or *Herald*, we should interpret it as the studied taunt of an enemy. Here it betrays a settled, deep-seated, and most heartfelt contempt.

Be it so. They have reason to despise us. For ages our antipathy to this same "English rule" has been apparent – our writhing under it is continual and convulsive; yet here we are with the yoke about our necks to this day, galling and stinging as ever. We loathe their dominion, and we submit to it. Outrage is followed by insult, and insult by robbery and bloodshed and *we* – why, we

"Must, like a whore, unpack our heart with words,
And fall a-cursing!"

If we pursue this theme, we may say that which we ought not to say, at least for the present. But let us calmly examine what chance England has of perpetuating her rule here by the means which she appears likely to employ.

The Irish people, always half starved, are expecting absolute Famine day by day; they know that they are doomed to months of a weed-diet next summer – that "hungry Ruin has them in the wind" – and they ascribe it, *unanimously*, not so much to the wrath of Heaven as to the greedy and cruel policy of England. Be it right or wrong, such is their feeling. They believe that the seasons as they roll are but ministers of English rapacity – that their starving children cannot sit down to their scanty meal but they see the harpy-claw of *England* in their dish. They behold their own wretched food melting in rottenness off the face of the earth; and they see heavy-laden ships, freighted with the yellow corn their own hands have sown and reaped, spreading all sail *for England*: they see it, and with every grain of that corn goes a heavy curse.

Here is one phase of Irish feeling that bodes ill for "English Rule."

Again – the people believe, no matter whether truly or falsely, that if they should escape the Hunger and the Fever, their lives are not safe from judges and juries. They do not look upon the law of the land as a terror to evil-doers and a praise to those who do well – they scowl on it as an engine of foreign rule, ill-omened harbingers of doom: they have a belief, universal throughout all Ireland, that while "the judges" are in any county the sun never shines there. In short, Ireland is disaffected, and every year, every day, adds to that disaffection and to the causes of it. We see no chance of the universal discontent being mitigated or changed; on the contrary, it grows fiercer and more reckless every day. We dislike the laws, we distrust the law-makers; we pray to Heaven to guard us from the law administrators.

But there is more yet. Hunger and hardship lead to crime – crime trifling in amount considering the desperate provocation, murders far less frightful than the terrible scenes of blood – those murders most foul, base, and unnatural, that we read of in the English papers; but still there is crime, and for the gnawing misery and oppression which produce that crime, Irishmen expect no relief from "English Rule." They count English Government as a potent ally of tyrannical landlords; to them, English Government personifies itself in the dragoons who ride them down – in the adverse jury-box – in the *detecting*, hard-swearing policeman. The plagues of their country, and enemies of their lives, they believe to be jails, juries, and policemen; and behold! those who deal out English Rule from the Imperial Parliament promise them more jails, more juries, more trials, and military patrols and detectives without number. We have put the case strongly, but not more strongly than the state of this country warrants. What is to be the issue of it we cannot well foresee; but of one thing we are very sure – Ireland will never, under any circumstance, be otherwise than disaffected towards "English Rule;"

paltry "boons" will not conciliate this people to it – no forest of bayonets will make them love it – no "concessions" that a British Minister would dare to propose will alter the feeling in the least, and coercion will only make it more bitter and deadly. The Irish people are tame and patient enough – too tame and too patient; but an Insurrection Act is not the way to "pacificate" them – it cannot pacificate them – it will not – it ought not – and, (we speak plainly,) *it shall not!*

The Famine Year

John Mitchel

***The Nation**, 19 June, 1847.*

Following preface from the appendix of Jail Journal:

In June, 1847, Mitchel sat down to write for the *Nation* a review of "Irish Guide Books" and out of the memories they awakened was begotten by the existent horror of the Famine – this, the most beautiful and terrible article that has ever come from the pen of an Irish journalist. In it the John Mitchel of 1848 has his birth.

Again, the great sun stands high at noon above the greenest island that lies within its ken on all the broad zodiac road he travels, and his glory, "like God's own head," will soon blaze forth from the solstitial tower. Once more, also – even in this June month of the rueful year – the trees have clothed themselves in their wonted pomp of leafy umbrage, and the warm air is trembling with the music of ten thousand singing-birds, and the great all-nourishing earth has arrayed herself in robes of glorious green – the greener for all the dead she has laid to rest within her bosom.

> What! Alive and so bold, O Earth!
> Art thou not over bold?
> What! Leapest thou forth as of old,

In the light of thy morning mirth?

Why, we thought that the end of the world was at hand; we never looked to see a bright, genial summer, a bright, rigorous winter again. To one who has been pent up for months, labouring with brain and heart in the panic-stricken city, haunted by the shadow of death, and has heard from afar the low, wailing moan of his patient, perishing brothers borne in upon every gale, black visions of the night well come swarming; to his dulled eye a pall might visibly spread itself over the empyrean, to his weary ear the cope of Heaven might ring from pole to pole with a muffled peal of Doom. Can such swinkt labourer believe that days will ever be wholesome any more, or nights ambrosial as they were wont to be? – for is not the sun in sick eclipse and like to die, and hangs there not upon the corner of the moon a vaporous drop profound, shedding plague and blight and the blackness of darkness over all the world?

Not so, heavy-laden labourer in the seed-field of time. Sow diligently what grain thou hast to sow, nothing doubting; for indeed, there shall be hereafter, as of old, genial showers and ripening suns, and harvests shall whiten, and there shall verily be living men to reap them, be it with sword or sickle. The sun is not yet turned into darkness, nor the moon into blood; neither is the abomination of desolation spoken of by Jeremy the Prophet yet altogether come to pass. Heaven and earth grow not old, as thou and thy plans and projects and speculations all will most assuredly do. Here have you been gnawing your heart all winter about the "state of the country," about a Railway Bill, about small rating districts, or about large; casting about for means to maintain your own paltry position; or else, perhaps, devising schemes, poor devil! for the regeneration of your country, and dreaming that in your own peculiar committee, clique, confederacy, caucus, council, conclave, or cabal, lay Ireland's last and only hope! – until you are nearly past hope yourself – until foul shadows are creeping over your light of life, and insanity is knocking at your parietal bone. Apparently you will be driven to this alternative – to commit suicide, or else, with a desperate rush, to fly into the country, leaving the spirits of evil and the whole rout of hell at the first running stream.

We advise the latter course; all the powers of nature enforce and conjure to it; every blushing evening woos thee westward; every blue morning sends its Favonian airs to search thee out in thy study and fan thy cheek, and tell thee over what soft, whispering woods; what bank of breathing field flowers; what heathery hills fragrant with bog myrtle and all the flora of the moors: what tracks of corn and waving meadows they have wandered before they came to mix with the foul city atmosphere, dim with coal smoke and the breath of multitudinous scoundreldom. On such blue morning, to us, lying wistfully dreaming with eyes wide open, rises many a vision of scenes that we know to be at this moment enacting themselves in far-off lonely glens we wot of. Ah! there is a green nook, high up amidst the foldings of certain granite mountains, forty leagues off and more, and there is gurgling through it, murmuring and flashing in the sun, a little stream clear as crystal — the mystic song of it, the gushing freshness of it, are even now streaming cool through our adust and too cineritious brain; and, clearly as if present in the body, we seek the grey rock that hangs over one of its shallow pools, where the sun rays are broken by the dancing water into a network of tremulous golden light upon the pure sand that forms its basin; and close by, with quivering leaves and slender stem of silver, waves a solitary birch-tree; and the mountains stand solemn around, and by the heather-bells that are breaking from their sheaths everywhere under your steps, you know that soon a mantle of richest imperial purple will be spread over their mighty shoulders and envelop them to the very feet. Lie down upon the emerald sward that banks this little pool, and gaze and listen. Through one gorge that breaks the mountain pass to the right hand, you see a vast cultivated plain, with trees and fields and whitened houses, stretching away into the purple distance, studded here and there with lakes that gleam like mirrors of polished silver. Look to the left, through another deep valley, and — lo! the blue Western Sea! And aloft over all, over land and sea, over plain and mountain, rock and river, go slowly floating the broad shadows of clouds, rising slowly from the south, borne in the lap of the soft, south wind, slowly climbing the blue dome by the meridian line, crossing the path of the sun, nimbus after nimbus, cirrus and cumulus, and every other cloud after his cloud, each flinging his mighty shadow on the passes, and then majestically melting off northward. What battalions and broad-winged hosts of clouds are these! Here have we lain but two hours, and there have been continually looming upward from behind the wind, continually sailing downward beyond the northern horizon, such wondrous drifts and piled up mountain of vapour as would shed another Noachian deluge and quench the stars if the floodgates were once let loose and the windows of heaven opened, yet this fragrant, soft-blowing southern gale bears them up bravely on its invisible pinions and softly winnows them on their destined way. They have a mission; they are going to build themselves up, somewhere over the Hebrides, into a huge, many-towered Cumulostratus; and to-morrow or the day after will come down in thunder and storm and hissing sheets of grey rain, sweeping the Sound of Mull with their trailing skirt, and making the billows of Corrievrechan seethe and roar around his cliffs and caves. Ben Cruachan, with his head wrapped in thick night, will send down Awe River in raging spate, in a tumult of tawny foam, and Morven shall echo through all his groaning woods.

But one cannot be everywhere at once. We are not now among the Western Isles, buffeting a summer storm in the Sound of Mull;

but here in this green nook, among our own Irish granite mountains, at our feet the clear, poppling water, over our head the birch leaves quivering in the warm June air; and the far-off sea smooth and blue as a burnished sapphire. Let the cloud-hosts go and fulfil their destiny; and let us, with open eye and ear and soul, gaze and listen. Not only are mysterious splendours around us, but mysterious song gushes forth above us and beneath us. In this little brook alone what a scale of notes! from where the first faint tinkle of it is heard far up as it gushes from the heart of the mountain, down through countless cascades and pools and gurgling rapids, swelling and growing till it passes our grassy couch and goes on its murmuring way singing to the sea; but it is only one of the instruments. Hark! the eloquent wind that comes sighing up the valley and whispering with the wavering fern! And at intervals comes from above or beneath, you know not which, the sullen croak of a solitary raven, without whose hoarse bass you never find nature's mountain symphony complete; and we defy you to say why the obscene fowl sits there and croaks upon his grey stone for half a day, unless it is that nature puts him in requisition to make up her orchestra, as the evil beast ought to be proud to do. And hark again! the loud hum of innumerable insects, first begotten of the Sun, that flit among the green heather stalks and sing all their summer life through — and then, if you listen beyond all that, you hear, faintly at first as the weird murmur in a wreathed shell, but swelling till it almost overwhelms all the other sounds, the mighty voice of the distant sea. For it is a peculiarity ever of this earth-music that you can separate every tone of it, untwist every strand of its linked sweetness, and listen to that and dwell upon it by itself. You may shut your senses to all save that far-off ocean murmur until it fills your ear as with the roar and rush of ten thousand tempests, and you can hear the strong billows charging against every beaked promontory from pole to pole; or you may listen to the multitudinous insect hum till it booms painfully upon your eardrum, and you know that here is the mighty hymn or spiritual song of life, as it surges ever upward from the abyss; louder, louder, it booms into your brain — oh, heaven! it is the ground-tone of that thunder-song wherein the earth goes singing in her orbit among the stars. Yes, such and so grand are the separate parts of this harmony; but blend them all and consider what a diapason! Cathedral organs of all stops, and instruments of thousand strings, and add extra additional keys to your pianofortes, and sweetest silver flutes, and the voices of men and of angels; all these, look you, all these, and the prima donnas of all sublunary operas, and the thrills of a hundred Swedish Nightingales, have not the compass nor the flexibility, nor the pathos, nor the loudness, nor the sweetness required for the execution of this wondrous symphony among the hills.

Loud as from numbers without number, sweet,
As of blest voices uttering joy.

Loud and high as the hallelujahs of choiring angels — yet, withal, what a trance of *Silence*? Here in this mountain dell, all the while we lie, breathes around such a solemn overpowering stillness, that the rustle of an unfolding heath-bell, too near breaks it offensively; and if you linger *near* enough — by heaven! you can hear the throb of your own pulse. For, indeed, the divine silence is also a potent instrument of that eternal harmony, and bears melodious part.

"Such concord is in heaven!" Yea, and on the earth, too, if only *we* — we who call ourselves the beauty of the world and paragon of animals — did not mar it. Out of a man's heart proceedeth evil thoughts; out of his mouth come revilings and bitterness and evil-speaking. In us, and not elsewhere, lies the fatal note that jars all the harmonies of the universe, and makes them like sweet bells jangled out of tune. Who will show us a way to escape from ourselves and from one another? Even, you, reader, whom we have invited up into this mountain, we begin to abhor you in our soul; you are transfigured before us; your eyes are become as the eyes of an evil demon, and now we know that this gushing stream of living water could not in a life-time wash away the iniquity from the chambers of thine heart; the arch-chemist sun could not burn it out of thee. For know, reader, thou hast a devil; it were better thy mother had not borne thee; and almost we are impelled to murder thee where thou liest.

"Poor human nature! Poor human nature!" So men are accustomed to cry out when there is talk of any meanness or weakness committed, especially by themselves; and they seem to make no doubt that if we could only get rid of our poor human nature we should get on much more happily. Yet human nature is not the worst element that enters into our composition — there is also a large diabolical ingredient — also, if we would admit it, a vast mixture of the brute, especially the donkey nature — and then, also, on the other hand, some irradiation of the godlike, and by that only is mankind redeemed.

For the sake whereof we forgive thee, comrade, and will forbear to do thee a mischief upon the present occasion. But note well how the very thought of all these discords has silenced, or made inaudible to us, all these choral songs of earth and sky. We listen, but there is silence — mere common silence; it is no use crying *Encore*! either the performers are dumb or we are stone deaf. Moreover, as evening comes on, the grass and heath grow somewhat damp, and one may get cold in his human nature. Rise, then, and we shall show you the way through the mountain to seaward, where we shall come down upon a little cluster of seven or eight cabins, in one of which cabins, two summers ago, we supped sumptuously on potatoes and salt with the decent man who lives there, and the black-eyed woman of the house and five small children. We had a hearty welcome though the fare was poor; and as we toasted our potatoes in the *greeshaugh*, our ears drank in the honey-sweet tones of the well-beloved Gaelic. If it were only to hear, though you did not understand, mothers and children talking together in their own blessed Irish, you ought to betake you to the mountains every summer. The sound of it is venerable, majestic, almost sacred. You hear in it the tramp of the clans, the judgment of the Brehons, the song of bards. There is no name for "modern enlightenment" in Irish, no word corresponding with the "masses," or with "reproductive labour"; in short, the "nineteenth century" would not know itself, could not express itself in Irish. For the which, let all men bless the brave old tongue, and pray that it may never fall silent by the hills and streams of holy Ireland — never until long after the great nineteenth century of centuries, with its "enlightenment" and its "paupers," shall be classed in its true category the darkest of all the Dark Ages.

As we come down towards the roots of the mountain, you may feel, loading the evening air, the heavy balm of hawthorn blossoms; here are whole thickets of white-mantled hawthorn, every mystic tree (save us all from fairy thrall!) smothered with snow-white and showing like branching coral in the South Pacific. And be it remembered that never in Ireland, since the last of her chiefs sailed away from her, did that fairy tree burst into such luxuriant beauty and fragrance as this very year. The evening, too, is delicious; the golden sun has deepened into crimson, over the sleeping sea, as we draw near the hospitable cottages; almost you might dream that you beheld a vision of the Connacht of the thirteenth century; for that —

> The clime, indeed, is a clime to praise,
> The clime is Erin's, the green and bland;
> And this is the time – these be the days –
> Of Cathal Mor of the Wine-Red Hand –

Cathal Mor, in whose days both land and sea were fruitful, and the yeanlings of the flocks were doubled, and the horses champed yellow wheat in the mangers.

But why do we not see the smoke curling from those lowly chimneys? And surely we ought by this time to scent the well-known aroma of the turf-fires. But what (may Heaven be about us this night) — what reeking breath of hell is this oppressing the air, heavier and more loathsome than the smell of death rising from the fresh carnage of a battlefield. Oh, misery! had we forgotten that this was the *Famine Year*? And we are here in the midst of those thousand Golgothas that border our island with a ring of death from Cork Harbour all round to Lough Foyle. There is no need of inquiries here — no need of words; the history of this little society is plain before us. Yet we go forward, though with sick hearts and swimming eyes, to examine the Place of Skulls nearer. There is a horrible silence; grass grows before the doors; we fear to look into any door, though they are all open or off the hinges; for we fear to see yellow chapless skeletons grinning there; but our footfalls rouse two lean dogs, that run from us with doleful howling, and we know by the felon-gleam in the wolfish eyes how they have lived after their masters died. We walk amidst the houses of the dead, and out at the other side of the cluster, and there is not one where we dare to enter. We stop before the threshold of our host of two years ago, put our head, with eyes shut, inside the door-jamb, and say, with shaking voice, "God save all here!" — No answer — ghastly silence, and a mouldy stench, as from the mouth of burial-vaults. Ah! they are dead! they are dead! the strong man and the fair, dark-eyed woman and the little ones, with their liquid Gaelic accents that melted into music for us two years ago; they shrunk and withered together until their voices dwindled to a rueful gibbering, and they hardly knew one another's faces; but their horrid eyes scowled on each other with a cannibal glare. We know the whole story — the father was on a "public work," and earned the sixth part of what would have maintained his family, which was not always paid him; but still it kept them half alive for three months, and so instead of dying in December they died in March. And the agonies of those three months who can tell? — the poor wife wasting and weeping over her stricken children; the heavy-laden weary man, with black night thickening around him — thickening within him — feeling his own arm shrink and his step totter with the cruel hunger that gnaws away his life, and knowing too surely that all this will soon be over. And he has grown a rogue, too, on those public works; with roguery and lying about him, roguery and lying above him, he has begun to say in his heart that there is no God; from a poor but honest farmer he has sunk down into a swindling, sturdy beggar; for him there is nothing firm or stable; the pillars of the world are rocking around him; "the sun to him is dark and silent, as the moon when she deserts the night." Even ferocity or thirst for vengeance he can never feel again; for the very blood of him is starved into a thin, chill serum, and if you prick him he will not bleed. Now he can totter forth no longer, and he stays at home to die. But his darling wife is dear to him no longer; alas! and alas! there is a dull, stupid malice in their looks: they forget that they had five children, all dead weeks ago, and flung coffinless into shallow graves — nay, in the frenzy of their despair they would rend one another for the last morsel in that house of doom; and at last, in misty dreams of drivelling idiocy, they die utter strangers.

Oh! Pity and Terror! what a tragedy is here — deeper, darker than any bloody tragedy ever enacted under the sun, with all its dripping daggers and sceptred palls. Who will compare the fate of men burned at the stake, or cut down in battle — men with high hearts and the pride of life in their veins, and an eye to look up to heaven, or to defy the slayer to his face — who will compare it with *this*?

No shelter here to-night, then: and here we are far on in the night, still gazing on the hideous ruin. O Batho! a man might gaze and think on such a scene, till curses breed about his heart of hearts, and the *hysterica passio* swells in his throat.

But we have twelve miles to walk along the coast before we reach our inn; so come along with us and we will tell you as we walk together in the shadows of the night.

To the Right hon. Lord John Russell, prime minister of the queen of england

John Mitchell

From The United Irishman (No. 10), 15 April, 1848.

MY LORD, – The Crown and Government of your gracious Sovereign Lady are, it seems, in danger, and want "further security." Security not against foreign enemies – for the Frenchman, the American, the very Russian bear, give assurances of friendly relations – but against her own beloved, highly-favoured, too-indulgently-used, but ungrateful, subjects! What is more wonderful, the danger arises not in the administration of those wicked Tories, – wretches obstructive of "human progress," the enemies of the human race, – but while you, even *you*, rule her Majesty's councils; *you*, the very high-priest of Liberality and Concession; *you*, who were to have ruled by justice, not coercion – opinion, not bayonets; whose thoughts were for ever intent on commercial reform, or municipal reform, or sanatory reform. What could a conciliatory Premier do (or promise) that you have not done (or promised)? Yet the very Crown and Constitution are in danger. May GOD be between us and harm!

And, what is strangest of all, it seems to be from the Irish that you fear this danger most; the people whom you have been nourishing, cherishing, and spoon-feeding, by means of so many kind and well-paid British nurses, for two years – on whom you have lavished so many tons of printed paper, so many millions of cooked rations – the exact number is it not written in the books of Bromley and the archives of the Union workhouses? – These are the people who plot "treason," and eagerly flock to hear "open and advised speaking," eagerly devour "published, printed, and written" language, all urging them to arm for the overthrow of British rule in Ireland! It is a bad world!

I fear that your Lordship, in your Whig complacency, has but a slender perception of the truth. Think of it a moment calmly. Here is this UNITED IRISHMAN newspaper, that your Lordship has been studying so attentively of late. It has reach only its tenth number; it was hardly advertised, and not puffed at all; it has been written ten with no extraordinary talent, has displayed, I muss confess, but little wit, and less brilliancy; – yet never a newspaper in Ireland reached such a circulation before in so short a time, and that circulation, remember, is amongst the very poorest of the people both in town and country; it is the very organ of pauperism; the public opinion it seeks to concentrate is that of the "Men of No Property" – *A Pauper Public Opinion!*

And why has it grown so popular? Why do poor men club their pence to buy it, and get it read to eager crowds every Saturday evening and Sunday morning? Why? – Because it utters for them the deep and inextinguishable hatred they all bear in their inmost souls against the "Crown and Government" of Britain; because it translates this holy hatred, never yet uttered, save in stifled curses and gnashing of teeth, into loud defiance, and hurls it weekly in the face of all your Viceroys, and Premiers, and Commanders-in-Chief; and especially because it points out the way, and the only true way, in which brave men ever win freedom or bridle tyrants, and exhorts them continually to rise out of the miserable slough of moral force wherein O'Connell plunged them, and stand erect with the words of freemen on their lips, and the Arms of freemen in their hands, defying "Law," trampling on Cant, and waging open war upon Humbug.

But you, the "Government," will not endure this sort of teaching! You will check it at all hazards: – if it cannot be stopped as a misdemeanour, you will make it "felony:" – if nothing else will do, the people of Ireland must be weaned from anarchists and "Jacobins" by taking the said Jacobins, chaining them in couples, cropping their heads, arraying them in grey jackets, and shipping them to the Antipodes!

And indeed, my lord, this "vigorous" policy will prove an effectual check upon us Irish "revolutionists," provided the men with whom you have to deal are fools, braggarts, traitors, and cowards. If we have undertaken the trade of patriotism for profit – if we have played the game of patriotism for notoriety – if we have been merely aspirants to the cheap martyrdom of two years' imprisonment, with *fetes*, and *levees*, and *couches* – why, in that case, the thing is at an end – you have tamed us, and fixed a bit between our teeth; – sedition is crushed, and the Queen's "Crown and Government" are safe for this time.

Or if we have made a gross and signal *mistake* as to the position, feeling, and necessities of our country – if we have not, after all, a nation at our back, but are merely isolated enthusiasts, *fugling* preposterously before imaginary troops – in this case, also, our game is over – we shall just get punished – all sensible men will say we deserve it; and there an end.

These issues will soon be tried, and I am glad of it. For twelve long months we have desired to see this day. Twelve months ago, on the Easter Monday of last year, Dublin saw one of the most ignominious Easter festivals – one of the ghastliest galas ever exhibited under the sun – the solemn inauguration, namely, of the Irish nation in its new career of national pauperism. There, in the esplanade before the "Royal Barrack," was erected the national model soup-kitchen, gaily bedizened, laurelled, and bannered, and fair to see; and in and out, and all around, sauntered parties of our supercilious second-hand "better classes" of the Castle-offices, fed on superior rations at the people's expense, and bevies of fair dames, and military officers, braided with public braid, and padded with public padding; and there, too, were the pale and piteous ranks of model-paupers, broken tradesmen, ruined farmers, destitute sempstresses, ranged at a respectful distance till the genteel persons had duly inspected the arrangements – and then marched by policemen to the place allotted them, where they were to feed on the meagre diet with *chained spoons* – to show the "gentry" how pauper spirit can be broken, and pauper appetite can gulp down its bitter bread and its bitterer shame and wrath together; – and all this time the genteel persons chatted and simpered as pleasantly as if the clothes they wore, and the carriages they drove in, were their own – as if "Royal barracks" Castle, and Soup-kitchen, were to last for ever.

We three criminals, my Lord, who are to appear to-day in the Court of Queen's Bench, were spectators of that soup-kitchen scene; and I believe we all left it with one thought, – that this day we had surely touched the lowest point – that Ireland and the Irish *could* sink no further; and that she must not see such another Easter Monday, though we should die for it.

My Lord, I came to the conclusion on that day that the Queen's "Crown and Government" were in danger – nay, that they ought to be in danger; – and I resolved that no effort of mine should be wanting to make the danger increase and become *critical*. As I looked on the hideous scene, I asked myself whether there were, indeed "law" or "Government" in the land – or if so, whether they were not worse than *no* law and *no* government. What had law done for these poor wretches and their five million fellow-paupers throughout Ireland? It was the "law" that carried off all the crops they raised, and shipped them to England; it was "law" that took the labour of their hands, and gave them half food for it while they were able to work; and cast them off to perish, like supernumerary kittens. "Law" told them they must not wear the cloth they wove, nor cut the corn they raised, nor dwell in the houses they builded; and if they dared do any of these things, or remonstrate against the hard usage, "Law" scourged and bullied them, imprisoned, gagged, and coerced them; to bring them to a more submissive mind. And what was more shameful and fatal still, this devoted people were in the hands of "leaders," who told them that all this "Law" – this London Parliament Law – was the law of God, – that if they violated it by eating the food they made, or wearing the cloth they wove, they committed a crime, and gave strength to the enemy – nay, those "leaders" never failed to thank God in public, with sanctimonious voice and head uncovered, that their fellow-countrymen *were* dying in patience and perseverance amidst their own bounteous harvests; Parliament Law was acknowledged as the supreme Ruler and Judge, and its decrees submitted to as the inscrutable dispensations of a Parliament Providence.

Such degradation was unexampled in the world. To think that Ireland was my country became intolerable to me. I felt that I had no right to breathe the free air or to walk in the sun; I was ashamed to look my own children in the face, until I should do something towards the overthrow of this dynasty of the Devil. And I resolved that Parliament Law must be openly defied and trampled on; and that I – if no other, even I – would show by countrymen how to do it. For I knew, my lord, that the monster, for all his loud roar and formidable tusks, was impotent against Truth and Right, – in other words that not Parliament Law, at bottom, but God's justice, ruled the earth. In short, I determined to walk, before the eyes of this downtrodden people, straight into the open jaws of "Law," to draw his fangs, to tear out his lying tongue, and to fling his carcase to be trampled on by those who had trembled at his nod.

I may be devoured, it is true. "Law" may be able to resist the first attack; and the three first assailants may fall: – yet shall we *do our business*. We may be destroyed; we will not be defeated.

You heard SMITH O'BRIEN on Monday last, amidst the howling of your Parliament mob, deliver Ireland's defiance; – think you this man will shrink from your new-made London "felony," or be gagged and frightened by your "bills" with their huge mob-majorities? But, perhaps, you imagine it was a mere display of individual contumely, or piqued vanity? – My lord, in every word, every syllable, every tittle that O'BRIEN promised or threatened on Monday night, he knew that he was uttering the inmost thoughts and feelings, the cordial hatred and defiance, of five million hearts; and it shall be made good to the letter. No more fortunate event has happened for Ireland than your selection of WILLIAM SMITH O'BRIEN and THOMAS FRANCIS MEAGHER to be treated as degraded criminals or dangerous lunatics; because these are precisely the men who will not blench before your judges, your bayonets, your juries, or your gibbets. What the People want to see in their leaders is individual heroism; is the determination to *do* themselves what they incite others to do; and seeing *that*, I believe they will follow, though it were to the gibbet's foot or the cannon's muzzle.

See, now, what it is you have undertaken to do! *First*, to crush and frighten men who have taken upon them a task like ours, moved by such motives, stirred by such passions, sustained by such determination, as I have described to you. *Second*, to stay discontent and disaffection by shutting the mouths who utter what all think and feel. On this latter point, I am surprised that your lordship's well-known learning as a political economist has not aided you. There is a *demand*, a brisk and increasing demand, for treason and sedition; you know demand (see ADAM SMITH) creates a supply. If THE UNITED IRISHMAN be removed, others will be found to furnish the article in any quantity that may be needed; and, indeed, I hereby advertise to all enterprising "Jacobins," that in Ireland there has been opened an altogether boundless market for this kind of ware; – that the article wanted is of the coarsest and strongest kind; – that ornaments and trimmings (as brilliant humour or tender poetry) are not absolutely necessary; – all that is required being good, sound, hearty, *bona fide* sedition, plain military instructions, sharp incentives to rebellion, strong treason, and thorough-going felony without benefit of clergy.

However, my lord, as you *have* undertaken this task – as you have deliberately pitted this British "law" against the Irish nation, there is one little matter I should like to arrange with you. I have already broached the subject to my LORD CLARENDON; but there is no use in talking to *him* – he is too hopelessly committed to bad company, and involved in evil courses. I mean, of course, the packing of the jury. Your lordship, however, is the author of a work on the

British constitution, and also (perhaps you forget it, as most other persons do, but I assure you that you are) of a memoir of Lord WILLIAM RUSSELL, your distinguished ancestor. It is mainly for the sake of refreshing your memory (and the public's) upon the subject of this memoir, that I have chosen to address my present letter to your lordship. You had great zeal thirty years ago for "constitutional liberty," and all that sort of thing (you may forget it, but I do assure you that you had) – and you tell, in this memoir, with becoming indignation, how that the Court, when it intended to shed the blood of the popular leaders, cheated the citizens of London of their rights, and got hold of the appointment of the sheriffs (this villainy was only temporary in London – it is a permanent institution of state in Dublin), and how the Court "soon had an opportunity of making use of their new power;" – how, "having shed the blood of Colledge, the Court next attempted the life of Lord SHAFTESBURY" (vol. ii. p. 6) – how the city was thronged with troops to intimidate the people; and how ROGER L'ESTRANGE, in the columns of *The Observator* (which was the name the *Times* then went by), declared "that a citizen's scull was but a thing to try the temper of a soldier's sword upon" – (vol. 2. p. 11.) You further narrate, my lord, how that when the bloodhounds at last pounced on Lord Russell, "after the examination was finished he was sent a close prisoner to the Tower. Upon his going in, he told his servant, TAUNTON, that he was sworn against, and that *they would have his life*. TAUNTON said, he hoped it would not be in the power of his enemies to take it. Lord Russell answered Yes; the Devil is loose (meaning that the Sheriff had his instructions.) From this moment he looked on himself as a dying man, and turned his thoughts wholly to another world. He read much in the Scriptures, particularly in the Psalms" – (vol. 2, p. 25.)

Truly, it was time for him to make his soul! But the trial came on; and "upon calling over the names, Lord Russell challenged no less than one-and-thirty; a fact which can hardly be explained," says your lordship "but by supposing that *some pains had been taken by his enemies in the selection.*" – p. 40. Your lordship may say that. But all his challenges were of no avail; his enemies had selected too skilfully; and they murdered him on Tower Hill.

In the Act of 1. William & Mary, annulling Lord Russell's attainder, it is recited, that he was convicted by means of "Undue and illegal returns of jurors."

It seems, then, that there was packing of juries in those days – a horrible scandal, when practised in England, and against so amiable a nobleman! But does not your lordship know that all these enormities, and worse, are regularly practised in Ireland down to the present day? Do you not know that in Dublin the Sheriff is *always* the creature of the Crown? And that he is created for this express purpose? Do you not know that your faction – I mean the English government – *never* got one verdict against a political offender, save from a well and skilfully packed jury? And that in the only case where they did *not* pack (viz., *The Queen against Duffy*, tried two years ago), they failed ignominiously.

The reason why they did not pack the jury in this case was, that they had been thoroughly shamed, and brought into disrepute by the monstrous fraud practised in the framing of the jury to try O'CONNELL and the Repeal Conspirators a short time before. They thought they could not repeat that trick so soon again; so they foolishly admitted three of the national party into the box.

I know, my lord, you will not commit that mistake again. I do not quote these passages from your lordship's book in the expectation that any silly weakness will prevail to make you give us a fair trial. I hope I know my place better; we are mere Irish; and I have not the presumptiont o imagine that *we* are entitled to as fair a jury as the noble British martyr, Lord WILLIAM RUSSELL. I have set these things down, therefore, not because I hope to produce any effect upon you, but because I know this letter will be read by (or read to) at least a hundred thousand men.

Of course, you will pack the jury against us, merely because all the world knows you dare not bring us to trial before an impartial jury of our countrymen. If you do, it will be the last criminal prosecution in Ireland at the suit of "our Lady the Queen" – as indeed, in any case, I trust it will be the last.

It matters little now whether you pack or do not pack. Whatever kind of trial you select – a fair one or a fraudulent – a trial for misdemeanour, or a trial for felony; – or whether you drop juries altogether, and try grape-shot, I tell you that *you are met*. The game is afoot; the work is begun; Ireland has now the "British Empire" by the throat; and if she relax his gripe till the monster is strangled, may she be a province, lashed and starved forever. Amen!

I remain, my Lord,
JOHN MITCHEL

P.S. – I find a sentence in your lordship's book (it is in vol. ii. p. 178), which it may be interesting to quote – not for you, my lord, but as before, for the aforesaid hundred thousand men. It is in these words: – "It is sufficient to justify the leaders of an insurrection that the people should be thoroughly weary of suffering, and disposed to view with complacency a change of rule." Very good.

J.M.

Jail Journal: Introduction

John Mitchel

ENGLAND has been left in possession not only of the soil of Ireland, with all that grows and lives thereon, to her own use. but in possession of the world's ear also. She may pour into, it what tale she will: and all mankind will believe her.

Success confers every right in this Enlightened Age; wherein, – for the first time, it has come to be admitted and proclaimed in set terms, that Success is Right and Defeat is Wrong; If I may profess myself a disbeliever in that gospel, the Enlightened Age will only smile, and say," The defeated always are." Britain being in possession of the floor, any hostile comment upon her way of telling our story is an unmannerly interruption; nay, is nothing short of an *Irish howl*.

And if Ireland be indeed conquered finally and irredeemably, it would be useless to importune the busy public (which has good heart enough, but really no time to attend to the grievances of mendicants), with any contradiction to the British story. – A touching and sanctimonious tale it is! – barbarian Celtic nature for ever revolting in its senseless, driftless way, against the genius of British civilisation – generous efforts for the amelioration of "that portion of the United Kingdom," met for ever by brutal turbulence, "crime and outrage," suspicion, ingratitude – British Benevolence stretching forth its open hand to relieve those same turbulent but now starving wretches, when Heaven smote the land with Famine – the anxieties, the cares, the expenses, that an unthrifty island cost her more prosperous sister, who would not, for ail that, desert her in her extremity, but would ameliorate her to the last.

So it runs; and so it might pass unchallenged for ever, if one could believe that the *last* conquest of Ireland was indeed the final and crowning conquest. But that Nation has been so often dead and buried, and has so often been born again – one and the same man sometimes both assisting at the rocking of her cradle, and as chief-mourner following her hearse, that there is no trusting to this seeming death. Mountjoy gave Ireland to Elizabeth, "Nothing but carcases and ashes," dead enough. In half a century, the carcases are armed men, the ashes flaming fire; and an Oliver Cromwell has to come over to smite and to slay again. Ireland was conquered by Cromwell, literally and universally. The cause of Ireland – Ireland as against England – was what all men would call *lost*: her castles rifted by the regicide's cannon; her fields laid waste, and the inheritance of them given to strangers; her best and bravest in bloody graves, or wasting and weltering in the Western Indies; – at her sister's feet she lay a corpse. A few years pass; she is not yet cold in her grave – and again all Europe hears the clang of aims in Ireland. Again the cause is Ireland against England, though the flags be the flags of Stuart against Orange-Nassau. Though the war-cry be *"Righ Seamus Abu!"* yet the war means Ireland for the Irish.

And again, a King and Deliverer of England comes over the sea to crush, kill, and trample Ireland – and again Ireland dies: on the Boyne stream her heart's blood runs to the sea; at the "Break of Aughrim" her neck is broken; and when the Wild Geese fly from

Limerick, England feels at last secure: surely this time her sister and mortal enemy is dead past all resurrection.

Not yet! Another gloomy and uneasy century drags along; the age of the Penal Laws. The English Government never yet observed any single treaty which it was convenient for them to break; and having solemnly agreed by the capitulation of Limerick not to impose penalties for Catholic worship, and having so disarmed the Catholic forces and ended the war, that Government, as a matter of course, at once imposed penal laws through their servile Anglo-Irish Parliament. Everybody has heard of the terrible *Penal Laws*; but not everybody knows what they were.

They took charge of every Catholic from his cradle, and attended him to his grave – Catholic children could only be educated by Protestant teachers at home; and it was highly penal to send them abroad for education.

Catholics were excluded from every profession, except the medical, and from all official stations without exception.

Catholics were forbidden to exercise trade or commerce in any corporate town.

Catholics were legally disqualified to hold leases of land for a longer tenure than thirty-one years; and also disqualified to inherit the lands of Protestant relatives.

A Catholic could not legally possess a horse of greater value than five pounds; and any true Protestant meeting a Catholic with a horse of fifty or sixty pounds in value, might lay down the legal price of five pounds, unhorse the idolator, mount in his place and ride away.

A Catholic child, turning Protestant, could sue his parents for maintenance; to be determined by the Protestant Court of Chancery.

A Catholic's eldest son, turning Protestant, reduced his father to a tenant for life, the reversion to the convert.

A Catholic priest could not celebrate Mass, under severe penalties; but any priest who recanted was secured a stipend by law.

Here was a code for the promotion of true religion; from whence it may appear, that Catholics have not been the only persecutors in the world. Some persons may even go so far as to say that no Catholic Government ever yet conceived in its heart so fell a system of oppression. However, it may be a circumstance in favour of the Protestant code (or it may not), that whereas Catholics have really persecuted for religion, enlightened Protestants only made a pretext of religion – taking no thought what became of Catholic souls, if only they could get possession of Catholic lands and goods. Alas, we may remark, that Catholic Governments, in their persecutions, always really desired the conversion of misbelievers (albeit their method was rough) – but in Ireland if the people had universally turned Protestant, it would have defeated the whole scheme.

Edmund Burke calls this Penal Code "a machine of wise and deliberate contrivance as well fitted for the oppression, impoverishment and degradation of a people, and the debasement in them of human nature itself, as ever proceeded from the perverted ingenuity of man." Singular, that it originated with the "Glorious Revolution," and was in full force during the reign of William the Deliverer, Anne, and the three first gracious Georges!

And it answered the purpose. The Irish people were impoverished and debased. And so the English, having forbidden them for generations to go to school, became entitled to taunt them with ignorance: and having deprived them of lands, and goods, and trade, magnanimously mock their poverty, and call them tatterdemalions.

During that eighteenth century, the Catholics disappear from history and politics. Such sallies of resistance as were made in those years against the encroachment of British power, were made by Protestants (Swift, Lucas, Molyneux), in assertion of a Protestant Nationality, and for the independence of a Protestant Parliament. Indeed, when the Protestant Dissenters of England argued for the repeal of the Corporation Act and Test Act, which prevented them from holding certain State offices, Dean Swift, the Irish patriot, wrote a sarcastic petition, as if from the Irish Catholics, praying that *they* might be relieved from their penal disabilities; in order to cast ridicule and discredit on the pretensions of Dissenters, by way of *reductio ad absurdum* – We will have the very Catholics, said he, coming in next!

We might well expect, by the close of that century, to find Ireland altogether Anglicised – the Catholics all dead or converted – the ruling classes so completely British in their feelings as well as by their extraction that England would never more need to fear the uprising of a hostile Irish Nation. Ireland was to all human appearance dead and buried this time.

And in truth so she might have lain for ever, if the English could have repressed their national greediness (or "energy") but a little. But it was impossible. The ruling class of Ireland, albeit Protestants, were soon taught that they were not to expect to be placed on an equal footing with men "whose limbs were made in England." Express enactments were made, to put an end to several branches of their trade, and to cramp and restrict others. Agriculture, too, which is the main concern of every nation, was accurately regulated in Ireland with a view to British interests. One hundred years ago, Ireland imported much corn from England; because it then suited the purpose of the other island to promote Irish sheep-farming in order to provide wool for the Yorkshire weavers. Tillage and cattle-feeding were discouraged; therefore the Irish were forbidden to export black-cattle to England. Sheep then became the more profitable stock, and the port of Barnstaple was opened to receive all their fleeces. But soon after, when England had full possession of the woollen manufacture, and that of Ireland was utterly ruined, it became apparent to the prudent British, that the best use they could make of Ireland would be to turn it into a general store-farm, for all sorts of agricultural produce.1 It is their store-farm to this day.

Those restrictive laws no longer exist. They have been repealed from time to time, merely because England wanted them no longer. The work was done; the British were in possession. To revive manufactures in Ireland, there must have been protective duties imposed on import of manufactured articles from England; but there was no free Irish Parliament to do this. Besides, the time became so enlightened that the Spirit of the Age was against such duties. In other words, the English could then afford to cry out "Free Trade!" "True principles of a political economy!" and-so-forth; taking care only to prevent any interference by law or otherwise, with the satisfactory state of things they had established. To lose a trade is easy; to recover it, in the face of wealthy rivals now in possession, impossible.

When manufactures are crushed, and a peasantry bound to the plough-tail and the cattle-shed, of course the manufactured commodities they require must come to them from abroad, and their raw agricultural produce must go in payment for them.

Further, when the condition of the peasantry is embittered by subjection to an alien and hostile class of landlords, who hold by lineage and affection to another country, and whose sole interest in their tenantry is to draw from them the very uttermost farthing, that they may spend it in that other country – and when that rental also, as well as the price of manufactures, must be paid in raw produce, the arrangement is as good as perfect. You can want no more to account for the starved skeletons of Ireland – and the comforts which brighten "the happy homes of England."

So went by the eighteenth century in Ireland. One can hardly believe that the sun shone as he is wont in those days.

So dreary and miserable is the landscape. – a good Bishop Berkeley putting these dismal queries in 1734 – "Whether there be upon earth any Christian or civilised people so beggarly, wretched, and destitute as the common Irish."- "Whether, nevertheless, there is any other people whose wants may be more easily supplied from home." Or writing thus to his friend, Prior, in Dublin – "The distresses of the sick and poor are endless. The havoc of mankind in the counties of Cork, Limerick and some adjacent places, have been incredible. The nation, probably, will not recover this loss in a century. The other day I heard one from the County of Limerick say that whole villages were entirely dispeopled. About two months since, I heard Sir Richard Cox say that five hundred were dead in the parish, though in a county, I believe not very populous"; – a bitter Dean Swift, with accustomed ferocity of sarcasm, while the *sæva indignatio* gnawed his heart, making and publishing his "Modest Proposal" to relieve the fearful distress by cooking and eating the children of the poor.

Yet, before the end of that same century – such vitality is there in the Irish race, and the Irish cause – Dublin streets beheld a wonderful spectacle – the Volunteer Army in its brilliant battalions, and an Independent Parliament legislating for the Sovereign Kingdom of Ireland! Apparently the conquest of Ireland had not yet been entirely finished.

For eighteen years, it seemed as if the steady progress of the British system in Ireland was about to be stopped or even turned back. The instinct and zeal of British "Amelioration," indeed, was as strong as ever, but 80,000 volunteer bayonets stopped the way. British statesmen were as desirous as ever to regulate in their minutest detail all the trade and traffic of Britain's sister island – surely for her sister's good – but on the muzzles of the Irish artillery was engraved the legend *"Free Trade or Else."*

During those eighteen years of Irish independence then, British policy was suspended. Honest John Bull all those years was losing a yearly income which he felt to be justly his due. Our countrymen began to manufacture again; and seditiously consumed their own corn and beef. Revenue expended in public improvements at home, to the prejudice of the British services – the metropolis of Dublin beautified and enriched, to the heavy loss of industrious Londoners – Irish landlords keeping their town-houses in Ireland and spending their rents at home, instead of paying rent and wages in England! The thing was not to be borne – and through "intolerance of Irish prosperity," preparations were made to conquer Ireland again by the Act of Union.

First, the Volunteers were to be disbanded and disarmed. Without that, no progress in civilisation could be made; nor could the British Providence carry out his wise designs. The disbanding was accomplished by pretending to grant fully (for the time) *all* that Ireland demanded. The too credulous people were taught that it would look suspicious if they kept up such an armament; and in an evil hour the Volunteers once more committed the defence of their island to her sister country.

Next, to frighten the gentry of Ireland into an Union, an insurrection had to be provoked. The expedients by which this was effected are known well enough; but the rebellion of '98, when it did burst out, had nearly proved too strong for its fomenters: and it needed General Lake with twenty thousand disciplined men, and complete batteries of field-artillery, to suppress it in the county of Wexford alone.

The noble owners of nomination boroughs were bribed, at £15,000 per borough, to sell them to the English Government.

The Catholic Bishops were bribed by promises of Emancipation (which the English delayed to fulfil for thirty years), to deliver over their flocks into the hands of the British.

The country was in abject terror; the Press was crushed by prosecutions; public meetings were dispersed by dragoons. The Irish Parliament was crowded (through the prudent bargaining of the noble owners of nomination boroughs) with English officers – in short, the year 1800 saw the *Act of Union*. At one blow, England had her revenge. Ireland, and all Irish produce and industry, were placed totally in her power; and Ireland having but one member in six to what, they called the Imperial Parliament, security was taken that the arrangement should never be disturbed.

This time, once more, Ireland was fully conquered – never nation yet took so much conquering and remained unsubdued. For twenty years after the Union the country was as absolutely prostrated in means and in spirit as she seems to be now; and as a matter of course she had her cruel famine every year. Without a famine in Ireland, England could not live as she had a right to expect; and the exact complement of a comfortable family dinner in England, is a coroner's inquest in Ireland: verdict, *Starvation*. In 1817 the famine was more desperate than usual, and in the best counties of Ireland, people fed on weeds. In 1822 it was more horrible still. Sir John Newport of Waterford, in his place in the House of Commons, described one parish in which fifteen persons had already died of hunger; twenty-eight more were past all hope of recovery, and one hundred and twenty (still in the same parish) ill of farriine-fever – and told of another parish where the priest had gone round and administered extreme unction to every man, woman, and child of his parishioners, *all* in *articulo mortis* by mere starvation.

All these years the Agricultural produce of Ireland was increasing more and more, and the English were devouring it. Indeed, so rapidly did this food-export (the only Irish commerce) grow and swell, that in 1826, to conceal the amount of it, the English Parliament placed it, "on the footing of a coasting-trade" – that is to say, no accounts were to be kept of it.

During the same period, every Parliament was sure to enact at least one Arms Bill; intending to deprive all mere Celts of necessary weapons for defence, and to kill in them the spirit of men.

Two distinct movements were all this while stirring the people; one open and noisy – the Catholic Relief Agitation, the other secret and silent – the Ribbon and White-boy movement. The first proposed to itself the admission of professional and genteel Catholics to Parliament and to the honours of the professions, all under London Law – the other, originating in an utter horror and defiance of London Law, contemplated nothing less than social, ultimately political *revolution*. For fear of the last, Great Britain with a very ill grace yielded to the first. Unfortunately for Ireland, Catholic Emancipation was carried in 1829. "Respectable Catholics" were contented, and became West Britons from that day.

At the head of that open and legal agitation, was a man of giant proportions in body and in mind; with no profound learning, indeed, even in his own profession of the law, but with a vast and varied knowledge of human nature, in all its strength, and especially in all its weakness; with a voice like thunder and earthquake, yet musical and soft at will, as the song of birds; with a genius and fancy, tempestuous, playful, cloudy, fiery, mournful, merry, lofty and mean by turns, as the mood was on him – a humour broad, bacchant, riant, genial and jovial – with profound and spontaneous natural feeling, and superhuman and superhuman passions, yet withal, a boundless fund of masterly affectation and consummate histrionism – hating and loving heartily, outrageous in his merriment, and passionate in his lamentation, he had the power to make other men hate or love, laugh or weep, at his good pleasure – insomuch that Daniel O'Connell, by virtue of being more intensely Irish, carrying to a more extravagant pitch all Irish strength and passion and weakness, than other Irishmen, led and swayed his people by a kind of divine, or else diabolic right.

He led them, as I believe, all wrong for forty years. He was a lawyer; and never could come to the point of denying and defying all British Law. He was a Catholic, sincere and devout; and would not see that the Church had ever been the enemy of Irish Freedom. He was an aristocrat, by position and by taste; and the name of a Republic was odious to him. Moreover, his success as a Catholic Agitator ruined both him and his country. By mere *agitation*, by harmless exhibition of numerical force, by imposing demonstrations (which are fatal nonsense), and by eternally half-unsheathing a visionary sword, which friends and foes alike knew to be a phantom – he had, as he believed, coerced the British Government to pass a Relief Bill, and admit Catholics to Parliament and some offices.

It is true that Sir Robert Peel and the Duke of Wellington said they brought in this measure, to avert civil war; but no British statesman ever officially tells the truth, or assigns to any act its real motive. Their real motive was, to buy into the British interests, the landed and educated Catholics; that so the great multitudinous Celtic enemy might be left more absolutely at their mercy.

For, beginning on the very day of Catholic Emancipation, there was a more systematic and determined plan of havoc upon the homes of the poor. First, the "forty-shilling freehold" was abolished. This low franchise for counties had induced landlords to subdivide farms, and to rear up population for the hustings. The franchise at an end, there was no political use for the people; and all encouragements and facilities were furnished by the British Government to get rid of them. Then began the "amelioration" (for benevolence guided all) of clearing off "surplus population," and consolidating the farms. It needed too much of the produce of the island to feed such a mob of Celts; and improved systems of tillage would give more com and cattle to English markets, more money to Irish landlords.

The code of cheap and easy Ejectment was improved and extended. All these statutes were unknown to the common law of England, and have been invented for the sole sake of the Irish Celt.

By an Act of the 25th year of George the Third (1815), in all cases of holdings where the rent was under £20 a year – that is, in the whole class of small tillage farms – power had been given to the County Judge at sessions, to make a decree for Ejectment at the cost of a few shillings. Two years afterwards, another Act was passed, which stated that in the proceedings under the former statute, "doubts had arisen" as to the admissibility, in certain cases, of the affidavit. of the landlord or lessor, or his agent, for ascertaining the amount due, and then proceeded to enact that such affidavits should be held sufficient. Under these two Acts, many an estate was cleared, many a farmer uprooted from his foothold in the soil, and swept out upon the highways: but yet not fast enough; so that by another Act of the first year of King George IV, it was declared that provisions of the cheap

Ejectment Act "*had been found highly beneficial,* and it was expedient that the same should be extended": and, thereupon, it was enacted by the King's most Excellent Majesty, by and with the advice, and-so-forth, that the power of summary Ejectment at Quarter Sessions should apply to all holdings at less than £50 rent; and, by the same statute, the cost of procuring these Ejectments was still further reduced. In the reigns of George IV and Victoria, other Acts for the same purpose were made. So that when the Famine and the Poor-laws came, the expense of clearing a whole countryside, was very trifling indeed. To receive some of the exterminated, Poor-houses were erected all over the island, which had the effect of stifling compunction in the ejectors. The Poor-houses were soon filled.

Yet all these years, from 1829 to 1846, with all the thinning and clearing, Celts kept increasing and multiplying. The more they multiplied, the more they starved; for the export of their food to England was also increasing yearly; then, with the greater demand for farms, rents rose and wages fell; and when at last the first shadow of the famine fell upon the island, nine-tenths of the people were living on the meanest and cheapest food, and upon a *minimum* of that.

But all these same years, loud and triumphant Agitations were going forward – the "Precursor" Agitation; the Repeal Agitation – and the cheers of imposing demonstrations rent the air. Our poor people were continually assured that they were the finest peasantry in the world – "Alone among the nations." They were told that their grass was greener, their women fairer, their mountains higher, their valleys lower, than those of other lands – that their "moral force" (alas!) had conquered before, and would again – that next year would be the Repeal year: in fine, that Ireland would be the first flower of the earth and first gem of the sea.

Not that the Irish are a stupid race, or naturally absurd, but the magician bewitched them to their destruction.

All these years, too, a kind of political war of posts was waged between O'Connell and British Ministers. Things called "good measures" were obtained; especially good men, friends and dependents of O'Connell's (for he was generous as the day) got offices. "Ameliorations" were now and then proposed – and if they were humbugs too manifest, O'Connell in his Hall, turned them inside out amidst laughter inextinguishable; and said "*Na bac leis*" and "Thank you for nothing, says the gallipot." Collateral issues all. Under all this, the heart and soul of Ireland – whatever of intellect and manliness was left in Ireland, beat and burned for independence – and England was skilfully laying her plans for the final conquest of her enemy.

For not one instant did the warfare cease upon farming Celts. In 1843, "Government" issued a notable commission; that is, appointed a few landlords, with Lord Devon at their head, to go through Ireland, collect evidence, and report on the best means (not of destroying the Irish enemy – official documents do not now use so harsh language, but) of ameliorating the relations of landlord and tenant in Ireland. On this commission, O'Connell observed that it was "a jury of butchers trying a sheep for his life," and said many other good things both merry and bitter, as was his wont; but the Devon Commission travelled and reported; and its Report has been the Gospel of Irish landlords and British Statesmen ever since.

Three sentences of their performance will show the drift of it. Speaking of "Tenant Right" (a kind of unwritten law whereby tenants in the North were secure from ejectment from their farms while they paid their rent, a custom many ages old, and analogous to the customs of farmers all over Europe), these Commissioners reported "that they foresaw some dangers to the just rights of property from the unlimited allowance of this tenant-right." On the propriety of consolidating farms (that is, destroying many small farmers to set up one large one), the Commissioners say, "When it is seen in the evidence, and in the return of the size of farms, how minute these holdings are, it cannot be denied that such a step is *absolutely necessary.*"

But the most remarkable sentence occurs in Lord Devon's "Digest of the Evidence," page 399:

"We find that there are at present 326,084 occupiers of land (more than one-third of the total number returned in Ireland), whose holdings vary from seven acres to less than one acre; and are, therefore, inadequate to support the families residing upon them. In the same table. No. 95, page 564, *the calculation is put forward,* showing that the consolidation of these small holdings up to eight acres, would require the *removal* of about 192,368 *families.*"

That is, the killing of a million of persons. Little did the Commissioners hope then, that in four years, British policy, with the famine to aid, would succeed in killing fully two millions, and forcing nearly another million to flee the country.

In 1846 came the Famine, and the "Relief Acts" advancing money from the Treasury, to be repaid by local assessment; and of course there was an aggravated and intolerable Poor-rate to meet this claim. Of which Relief Acts, only one fact needs to be recorded here – that the Public Works done under them were strictly ordered to be of an unproductive sort – that is, such as would create no fund to repay their own expenses. Accordingly, many hundreds of thousands of feeble and starving men were kept digging holes, and breaking up roads – doing not only no service, but much harm. Well, then, to meet these Parliamentary advances there was nothing but *rates*: and, *therefore*, there was the higher premium to landlords on the extermination, that is the slaughter, of their tenantry. If the clearing business had been active before, now there was a rage and passion for it; and as if the Cheap Ejectment Acts were not a speedy enough machinery, there was a new Poor-law enacted, containing amongst other clauses, the "Quarter Acre clause," which provided that if a farmer, having sold all his produce to pay the rent duties, rates and taxes, should be reduced, as many thousands of them were, to apply for public out-door relief, he should not get it until he had first delivered up all his land to the landlord. Under that law it is the able-bodied idler only who is to be fed – if he attempt to till but one rood of ground, he dies. This simple method of ejectment was called "passing paupers through the workhouse" – a man went in, a pauper came out.

Under these various Poor-laws and Relief Acts, there were at least 10,000 government offices, small and great; looking and canvassing for these were 100,000 men; a great army in the interest of England.

At the end of six years, I can set down these things calmly; but to see them might have driven a wise man mad. There is no need to recount how the Assistant Barristers and Sheriffs, aided by the Police, tore down the roof-trees and ploughed up the hearths of village after village – how the Quarter Acre clause laid waste the parishes, how the farmers and their wives and little ones in wild dismay, trooped along the highways – how in some hamlets by the seaside, most of the inhabitants being already dead, an adventurous traveller would come upon some family eating a famished ass – how maniac mothers stowed away their dead children to be devoured at midnight – how Mr. Darcy of Clifden, describes a humane gentleman going to a village near that place with some crackers, and standing at the door of a house; "and when he threw the crackers to the children (for he was afraid to enter), the mother attempted to take them from them" – how husband and wife fought like wolves for the last morsel of food in the house; how families, when all was eaten and no hope left, took their last look at the Sun, built up their cottage doors, that none might see them die nor hear their groans, and were found weeks afterwards, skeletons on their own hearth; how the "law" was vindicated all this while; how the Arms Bills were diligently put in force, and many examples were made; how starving wretches were transported for stealing vegetables by night; how overworked coroners declared they would hold no more inquests; how Americans sent corn, and the very Turks, yea, negro slaves, sent money for alms; which the British Government was not ashamed to administer to the "sister country"; and how, in every one of these years, '46, '47, and '48, Ireland was exporting to England, food to the value of fifteen million pounds sterling, and had on her own soil at each harvest, good and ample provision for double her own population, notwithstanding the potato blight.

To this condition had forty years of "moral and peaceful agitation" brought Ireland. The high aspirations after a national Senate and a national flag had sunk to a mere craving for food. And for food Ireland craved in vain. She was to be taught that the Nation which parts with her nationhood, or suffers it to be wrested or swindled from her, thereby loses all. O'Connell died heart-broken in 1847 – heart-broken not by a mean vexation at seeing the power departing from him; the man was too great for that; but by the sight of his People sinking every day into death under their inevitable, inexorable doom. His physicians ordered him to a warmer climate: in vain: amidst the reverent acclamations of Paris, through the sunny valleys of France, as he journeyed southward, that Banshee wail followed him and found him, and rung in his dying ear. At Genoa he died: ordering that the heart should be taken out of his dead body, and sent, not to Ireland, but to Rome; a disposition which proves how miserably broken and debilitated was that once potent nature.

Politics, by this time, was a chaos in Ireland. "Conciliation Hall" was sending forth weekly an abject howl for *food! food!* The "Irish Confederation" (of which the present writer was a member) had no much clearer view through the gloom; though it had more energy and honesty. Two or three vain efforts were made by its leaders to put a good man into the representation (Meagher at Waterford), or to keep a bad man out (Monahan at Galway) – both efforts in vain. The representation and the franchise were too cunningly calculated for British interests.

Every week was deepening the desolation and despair throughout the country; until at last the French Revolution of February, '48, burst upon Europe. Ireland, it is true, did not then possess the physical resources or the high spirit which had "threatened the integrity of the Empire" in '43; but even as she was, depopulated, starved, cowed and corrupted, it seemed better that she should attempt resistance, however heavy the odds against success, than lie prostrate and moaning as she was. Better that men should perish by the bayonets of the enemy than by their laws.

Clubs were formed expressly for arming; rifles were eagerly purchased; and the blacksmiths' forges poured forth pikeheads. Sedition, treason, were openly preached and enforced; and the United Irishman was established specifically as an Organ of Revolution. The Viceroy, Lord Clarendon, became alarmed: he concentrated eight thousand troops in Dublin; he covered the land with detectives; and informers were the chief frequenters of the Castle. Walls were covered with placards (printed by Thom, the Government Printer), warning peaceable citizens that "Communists" intended to rob their houses, and murder their families; detectives went to unsuspecting blacksmiths and mysteriously ordered pikes for the "revolution" – then brought the pikes to the Castle; and thereupon Lord Clarendon had additional reasons to call for more regiments from England, to mount cannon upon the Bank; to garrison the College; to parade his artillery through the streets. But this was not enough: his Lordship wanted an organ at the press; for it happened that, about that time, all the decent journals of the country were pouring contempt upon him and his government, except the *Dublin Evening Post*, which was bribed with public money. It was necessary to secure another organ. The cause of "Law and Order" – the interests of civilisation – the wise designs of a British Providence required more support. There was then in Dublin a paper of the most infamous character; a paper that subsisted upon hush-money (the only one of the sort ever printed in Ireland); a paper that was never quoted, whose name was never named by any Journal in the city. Its editor, an illiterate being of the name of Birch, had been prosecuted more than once, convicted at least once, and imprisoned six months, for procuring money from timid citizens by threats of publishing disgusting stories of their private life. To this man my Lord Clarendon applied, that he might aid him with his counsel and with his pen. With him he consulted at the Viceregal Lodge upon the critical posture of affairs, and upon the best mode of carrying out the designs of Providence for Ireland. In order the more effectually to do this pious work, it was needful that the avowed enemies of that British Providence (of whom the present writer had the honour to be one) should be covered with obloquy, and pointed out to the execration of mankind as abominable; but seeing that reputable persons never saw the Viceroy's new organ, it became necessary to circulate it gratuitously by means of public money.

Under the advice of this Birch, who told the Viceroy that it was time for *vigour*, his Lordship called for a new Law of Treason. Immediately (April 19th) a Bill was brought in by Sir George Grey, and made into an Act by large majorities, providing that any one who should levy war against the Queen, or endeavour to deprive her of her title, or by open and advised speaking, printing, or publishing, incite others to the same, should be "deemed guilty of felony" and transported.

This act was passed with a special view to crush the *United Irishman,* and to destroy its Editor. If the offence had been left a misdemeanour as theretofore, the "government" knew that the *United Irishman* could not be put down, because there would have been no *forfeiture* in case of conviction; and they were all well aware that competent men would not be wanting to give a voice to treason, even though editor after editor should be chained up.

In the meantime the case grew pressing. All the country was fast becoming aroused; and many thousands of pikes were in the hands of the peasantry. The soldiers of several regiments, being Irish, were well known to be very willing to fraternise with the people, upon a first success and the police, in such an event, would have been a green-coated Irish army upon the moment.

Birch and Clarendon would not even wait to get their enemy fairly into the new felony. They caused three to be arrested in the meantime (O'Brien, Meagher, and the present writer), on a charge of sedition; but on bringing the two former to trial, it was found that the juries (special juries in the Court of Queen's Bench) had not been closely enough packed; and the prosecutions failed. In my case, though there were two indictments, one for a speech, and one for an article, and two juries had actually been struck, "Government" felt that a failure would be at least dangerous; so the Viceroy suddenly caused my arrest on a charge of "treason-felony" under his new Act, and determined to, not try, but pretend to try me, at the next

Commission in Green Street – at any rate to clear Ireland of me and so get rid of one obstacle at least to the fulfilment of British policy.

Here, then, this narrative leaves the general affairs of the country and shrinks to the dimensions of a single prosecution. From the day that I entered my dungeon (the 23rd of May, 1848), I know but by hearsay how the British Government fulfilled the designs and administered the dispensations of Providence in Ireland – how the Famine was successfully *exploited*; how the Poor-rates doubled and trebled, and were diligently laid out in useless works; how the Orange Lodges were supplied with arms from the Castle; how the mere Celtic peasantry were carefully deprived of all weapons; how the land lords were gradually broken and impoverished by the pressure of rates, until the beneficent "Encumbered Estates Bill" had to come in and solve their difficulties – a great stroke of British policy, whereby it was hoped (now that the tenantry were cleared to the proper point) to clear out the landlords, too, and replace them with English and Scottish purchasers. In short, how the last conquest was consummated, let other pens than mine describe.

The *United Irishman* was at that time admitted to be making progress in stimulating the just disaffection of the people to the point of insurrection. The first and most earnest efforts, therefore, of the enemy's Government were now to be exerted for its destruction. And now came the momentous question of the jury. The Ministry of England happened to be a Whig Ministry; and one of the artifices by which the Whigs had gained their reputation for "liberality" was hypocritically censuring the Tories for *packing juries* – that is, carefully selecting their own friends apparently to try, but really to destroy a political enemy. I provoked them to this prosecution with the idea that if they did not pack, and were beaten on the trial (in a case of so open and flagrant "treason"), the *prestige* and the real power of the British rule in Ireland would be wounded seriously, perhaps mortally – but that if they broke through all Whig maxims, and obtained their conviction by the usual villainous means of excluding five-sixths of the people from serving on juries, the atrocity would still more exasperate the furious disaffection, and ripen the Revolution. In all this I under-estimated, on the one hand, the vigour and zeal of the British Government in carrying out the designs of Providence, and on the other, the much-enduring patience and perseverance of the Irish Catholics.

The day of trial approached; and it became well known in Dublin, that Lord Clarendon was resolved. Whig or no Whig, to pack at least this one jury most jealously. The juries to try O'Brien and Meagher had been selected, indeed, with considerable care; yet on each of those juries there had been left at least one friend of the national cause – a piece of official negligence which ended in the defeat of those prosecutions; and it was, therefore, clear that it must not be repeated. Just before my pretended "trial," however. Ministers were taken to task about the instructions which had been sent to Ireland for the conduct of the State prosecutions; and returns were moved for Lord John Russell replied, in a most virtuous speech, that nothing could be further from the intention of the Government than excluding Catholics as such, from the jury-box, using "unfairness," or turning the administration of justice into a matter of politics. The report of that virtuous speech arrived in Dublin on the very day when the Crown prosecutors and Attorney General were packing the jury, to convict me, as never jury was packed before – excluding all Catholics, as such – excluding all Protestants who were not *known* to be my enemies – openly "using unfairness," and using the false pretence of law and justice to crush a political enemy. There was not, of course, a single Catholic left upon this pretended jury; nor a single Protestant who was not well known to be for the Castle, and against the People.

Two or three days *after* my pretended trial – as I find in the papers – the same Lord John Russell, being questioned again by Mr. Keogh on the explusion of Catholics on all the three trials, declared that in the case of Mr. O'Brien and Mr. Meagher, jurors had not been set aside for political or religious opinions; but, said his Lordship, "*have no explanation to offer* with respect to what has taken place on the trial of Mr. Mitchel."

In short, the cause of "civilisation" and of British Law and Order, required that I should be removed to a great distance from Ireland, and that my office and printing materials should become the property of Her Majesty. Though the noble old Robert Holmes, who advocated the prisoner's cause that day, had had the tongue of men and of angels, he could have made no impression there. A verdict of "Guilty," and a sentence of fourteen years' transportation had been ordered by the Castle: and it was done.

The Clubs of Dublin, as I was credibly informed, were vehemently excited; and the great majority of them were of opinion that if an insurrection were to be made at all, it should be tried then and there – that is, in Dublin streets, and on the day of my removal. There is no reason why I should not avow that I shared in that opinion, and refused to sign a paper that was brought to me in Newgate, deprecating all attempt at rescue. I believed that if the City of Dublin permitted any Irishman to be put on board a convict-ship under such circumstances, the British Government could have little to fear from their resentment or their patriotism afterwards. Others of my Confederate comrades differed from me; restrained the Clubs; promised action in the harvest (a promise which they afterwards fulfilled to the best of their ability); bade me farewell mournfully enough; and in due course of time, some of them followed me on my circumnavigation of the globe.

Their decision was wrong; and, as I firmly believe, fatal. But that their motives were pure, and their courage unquestionable, I am bound to admit.

So much I have thought fit to narrate by way of Introduction to the diary which I kept in my cell. The general history of a nation may fitly preface the personal memoranda of a solitary captive; for it was strictly and logically a *consequence* of the dreary story here epitomised, that I came to be a prisoner, and to sit writing and musing so many months in a lonely cell. "The history of Ireland," said Meagher to his unjust judges at Clonmel, "explains my crime and justifies it." No man proudly mounts the scaffold, or coolly faces a felon's death, or walks with his head high and defiance on his tongue into the cell of a convict-hulk, *for nothing*. No man, let him be as "young" and as "vain" as you will, can do this in the wantonness of youth or the intoxication of vanity.

My preface, then, will explain, at least to some readers, what was that motive, spirit and passion which impelled a few Irishmen to brave such risks, and incur so dreadful penalties for the sake of but one chance of rousing their oppressed and degraded countrymen to an effort of manful resistance against their cruel and cunning enemy.

It will further help to explain the contumacy and inveterately rebellious spirit evident enough in the pages of the "Journal"; and, moreover, will suggest some of those considerations which lead the present writer to differ from the vast majority of mankind, and to assert that his native country has not been, even this time, finally subdued; that this earth was not created to be civilised, ameliorated and devoured by the Anglo-Saxons; that Defeat is not necessarily Wrong; that the British Providence is not Divine; and that *his* dispensations are not to be submitted to as the inscrutable decrees of God.

Clearing Decks

James Fintan Lalor

(The Irish Felon, No. 5)

It is never the mass of a people that forms it real and efficient might. It is the men by whom that mass is moved and managed. All the great acts of history have been done by a very few men. Take half a dozen names out of any revolution upon record, and what would have been the result?

Not Scotland but Wallace barred and baffled Edward. Not England but Cromwell struck a king from his seat. Not America, but six or eight American men, put stripes and stars on the banner of a nation. To quote examples, however, is needless. They must strike at once on every mind.

If Ireland be conquered now—or what would be worse still, if she fails to fight—it will certainly not be the fault of the people at large—of those who form the rank and file of the nation. The failure and fault will be that of those who have assumed to take the office of commanding and conducting the march of a people for liberty, without perhaps having any commission from nature to do so, or natural right, or acquired requisite.

The general population of this island are ready to find and furnish everything which can be demanded from a mass of a people—the numbers, the physical strength, the animal daring, the health, hardihood, and endurance. No population on earth of equal amount would furnish a more effective military conscription.

We want only competent leaders—men of courage and capacity—men whom nature meant and made for leaders—not the praters, and pretenders, and bustling botherbys of the old agitation. Those leaders are yet to be found. Can Ireland furnish them? It would be a sheer and absurd blasphemy against nature to doubt it. The first blow will bring them out.

But very many of our present prominent leaders must first retire to be dismissed. These men must first be got rid of utterly. They *must*. There is nothing else for it. They are stopping our way, clinging round our arms, giving us up to our enemies. Many came into this business from the mere desire of gaining a little personal distinction on safe terms and at a cheap and easy rate—of obtaining petty honours and offices—of making a small Dublin reputation—of creating a parish fame, or a tea-table fame.

They will never suffer the national movement to swell beyond the petty dimensions which they are able themselves to manage and command; and are, therefore, a source not of strength but of weakness—and the source of all our weakness. But for them we could walk down the whole force of England in one month.

In a movement of the nature of that which has been going on for years in this country, it was impossible to prevent the intrusion into offices of command or that class of men who mar success instead of making it. Indeed it was into their hands those offices have been almost exclusively confided up to the present hour. This can hardly be called a mistake for it was unavoidable. The movement naturally, and of necessity, belonged to them. It was of the mock heroic order, the machinery of which none but mean hands would undertake or be competent to manage.

The class of men who make revolutions, and who doubtless exist here as well as elsewhere, have been altogether disgusted and driven away from the service of their country by the peculiar character of that sort of "struggle for freedom" the system of "moral agitation" which Ireland thought fit to adopt, and from which their pride of manhood and pride of country revolted.

The staff of leaders which that system created and has left behind it is composed of men utterly unfit and unwilling to take charge of a military struggle, and who ought at once to be superseded and replaced. For two generations—may history forget to mention them—those men have been working to do this—the best work that ever yet was done for tyranny—to take from the people the terror of their name and make popular movement a mockery.

And what now are they working to do? To hold Ireland down hand and foot while her chains are being locked and double-locked, and her four noble prisoners sent fettered and handcuffed to a penal colony of England, and—hear it, O Earth, and hear it, O God! for saying that Ireland should suffer famine no more.

Oh! worse for us than the foreign tyrant is the native traitor; and worse than the open traitor in the enemy's ranks is the vile trickster and the base craven in our own. Away with them! They must quit at once or be quashed. One man, and every man, of those now in the prison of Newgate is worth a host of the dastards and drivellers who are bidding you stand by and "bide your time," while your best and bravest are being transported as felons in the face of your city, in the sight of two islands, and in view of all the earth.

But how are you to know them, these menials of England in the green livery of their country? By this shall ye know them. Any man who objects to every plan of armed resistance that is proposed, while he produces none or no better of his own. Or any man who tells you that any act of armed resistance—even if made so soon as tomorrow—even if offered by ten men only—even if offered by ten men armed only with stones—any man who tells you that such an act of resistance would be premature, imprudent, or dangerous—any and every such man should at once be spurned and spat at.

For, remark you this and recollect it, that *somewhere, somehow,* and by *somebody,* a *beginning must* be made; and that the *first* act of resistance is always, and must be ever premature, imprudent, and dangerous. Lexington was premature, Bunker's Hill was imprudent, and even Trenton was dangerous.

There are men who speak much to you of prudence and caution, and very little of any virtue beside. But every vice may call itself by the name of some virtue or other; and of prudence there are many sorts. Cowardice may call itself, and readily pass for, caution, and of those who preach prudence, it behoves to enquire what kind of prudence it is they speak of, and to what class of prudent persons they belong themselves. There is a prudence the virtue of the wisest and bravest—there is a prudence the virtue of beggars and slaves.

Which class do those belong to who are prating now for prudence, and against premature insurrection; while rejecting every proceeding and plan for preparation?

Against the advice of those men, and all men such as they, I declare my own. In the case of Ireland now there is but one *fact* to deal with, and *one question* to be considered. The fact is this—that there at present in occupation of this country some 40,000 armed men, in the livery and service of England; and the question is—how best to kill and capture those 40,000 men.

If required to state my own individual opinion, and allowed to choose my own time, I certainly would take the time when the full harvest of Ireland shall be stacked in the haggards. But not infrequently *God* selects and sends his own seasons and occasions; and oftentimes, too, an enemy is able to force the necessity of either fighting or failing.

In the one case we ought not, in the other we surely cannot, attempt waiting for our harvest-home. If opportunity offers, we must dash at that opportunity—if driven to the wall, we must wheel for resistance. Wherefore, let us fight in September if we may—but sooner if we must.

Meanwhile, however, remember this—that somewhere, and somehow, and by somebody, a beginning must be made. Who strikes the first blow for Ireland? Who draws first blood for Ireland? Who wins a wreath that will be green for ever?

To Charles Gavan Duffy, Editor of the "Nation."

James Fintan Lalor

Tenakill, Abbeyleix, January 11th, 1847

I am one of those who never joined the Repeal Association or the Repeal Movement—one of Mr. O'Connell's "creeping, crawling, cowardly creatures"—though I was a Repealer in private feeling at one time, for I hardly know that I can say I am one now, having almost taken a hatred and disgust to this my own country and countrymen.

I did not join the agitation, because I saw—not from reflection, but from natural instinct, the same instinct that makes one shrink from eating carrion—that the leaders and their measures, means, and proceedings, were intrinsically and essentially, vile and base; and such as never could or ought to succeed.

Before I embarked in the boat I looked at the crew and the commander; the same boat which you and others mistook in '43 for a war-frigate, because she hoisted gaudy colours, and that her captain swore terribly; I knew her at once for a leaky collier-smack; with a craven crew to man her, and a sworn dastard and foresworn traitor at the helm—a fact which you and Young Ireland would seem never to have discovered until he ordered the boat to be stranded, and yourselves set ashore.

I would fain become one of the "National" party, if they could consent to act along with me and I with them. But I confess I have my many doubts—I have had them all along; and they have been terribly strengthened by the two last numbers of the *Nation*. I mean those of December 26 and January 2; the last (January 9) I have not yet seen. It is not figure, but fact, that reading those two numbers made me ill.

I have long been intending to write to you to resolve those doubts, and have only been prevented by sickness. I must now defer doing do so for some little time longer, and my reason for writing this present hurried note is this: it has just occurred to me that, at the meeting on Wednesday, an Association may possibly be formed on such a basis, and resolutions or pledges adopted of such a character, as would exclude and excommunicate me and many beside.

These resolutions or pledges may relate either—1st, to the end; 2nd, to the means. Now remark—1st, As to the end: – Should the end be defined strictly, in terms or effect, to the Repeal—simple Repeal, and nothing but or besides Repeal—I would thereby be excluded. For, in the first place, I will never contribute one shilling, or give my name, heart, or hand, for such an object as the simple Repeal by the British Parliament of the Act of Union.

I shall state my reasons hereafter, not having time now. Don't define the object, nor give it such a name as would define it. Call it by some general name—independence, if you will—and secondly, I will never act with, nor aid any organisation limiting itself strictly to the sole object of dissolving the present connection with Britain and rigidly excluding every other. I will not be fettered and handcuffed.

A mightier question is in the land—one beside which Repeal dwarfs down into a petty parish question; one on which Ireland may not alone try her own right, but try the right of the world; on which you would be, not merely an asserter of old principles, often asserted, and better asserted before her, an humble and feeble imitator and follower of other countries—but an original inventor, propounder, and propagandist, in the van of the earth, and heading the nations; on which her success or her failure alike, would never be forgotten by man, but would make her, for ever, the lodestar of history; on which Ulster would be not "on her flank," but at her side, and on which, better and best of all, she need not plead in humble petitions her beggarly wrongs and how beggarly she bore them, nor plead any right save the right of her might.

And if the magnitude and magnificence of that other question be not apparent and recognised—any more than the fact on its settlement now depends the existence of an old and not utterly worthless people—it is partly, indeed, because the mass of mankind see all such questions, at first, through a diminishing glass, and every question is little until some one man makes it great; but partly, also, because the agitation of the Repeal question has been made to act as a proscription of every other.

Repeal may perish with all who support it soon than I will consent to be fettered on this question, or to connect myself with any organised body that would ban or merge in favour of Repeal or any other measure, that greatest of all our rights on this side of heaven, God's grant to Adam and his poor children for ever, when He sent them from Eden in His wrath and bid them go work for their bread. Why should I name it?

National independence, then, in what form of words you please; but denounce nothing—proscribe nothing—surrender nothing, more especially of your own freedom of action. Leave yourselves free individually and collectively.

2nd, As to the means:—If any resolution or pledge be adopted to seek legislative independence by moral force and legal proceedings alone, with a denunciation or renunciation of all or any other means or proceedings, you may have millions of better and stronger men than I have to join you; but you won't have me.

Such pledge, I am convinced, is not necessary to legalise any association. To illegalise there must, I conceive, be positive evidence of act or intention -deeds done or words spoken. Omitting to do anything can surely form no foundation for a legal charge. What! Is silence a proof of criminal intention? I speak, of course, in ignorance, being no lawyer, thank God!

But whether I be correct or not, I will never subscribe or assent to any such pledge or resolution. As regards the use of none but legal means, any means and all means might be made illegal by Act of Parliament; and such pledge, therefore is passive obedience. As to the pledge of abstaining from the use of any but moral force, I am quite willing to take such pledge if, and provided, the English Government agree to take it also; but "if not, not."

Let England pledge not to argue the question by the prison, the convict-ship, or the halter; and I will readily pledge not to argue it in any form of physical logic. But dogs tied and stones loose is no bargain. Let the stones be given up; or unmuzzle the wolf-dog.

There is one at this moment in every cabin throughout the land, nearly fit already to be untied—and he will be savager by-and-by. For Repeal, indeed, he will never bite, but only bay; but there is *another* matter to settle between us and England. There has already, I think, been too much giving in on this question of means and force.

Merely to save or assert the abstract right for the use of other nations or other times, won't do for me. We must save it for our own use, and assert it too, if need be, and occasion offer. You will receive, and, I hope, read this on tomorrow morning, before the Committee meet.

My petition to you is that you will use your influence from being adopted, which would cut me off from co-operating with the new Association, should one be founded. Don't mention my name. It is not one worth half a farthing; but such as it is I don't choose to give it to the Seceders until I have some better guarantee than I possess as yet, that their new organisation will be anything better, stronger, or nobler than a decently conducted Conciliation Hall, free from its open and brazen profession of meanness, falsehood, cowardice, and corruption, but essentially just as feeble, inefficient and ridiculous.

Is there any apology required for addressing you in this manner? I don't know. Perhaps I have no right—though I have been a Seceder since I ceased to be a child. I owe to you some gratitude. *You have given me a country.* Before your time I was an alien and an exile, though living in my own land. I hope you won't make me one again.

This letter has been hastily written; and I have not acquired the faculty of expressing what I wish with clearness or facility. Still I hope you will understand, or at least that you will not misunderstand me. The *Nation* of last Saturday might possibly give me information which would render my writing plainly unnecessary, but I don't receive it until Wednesday, being in partnership with another person—I remain, your obedient servant,

JAMES F. LALOR

A new naτιοn

James Fintan Lalor

Proposal for an Agricultural Association between the Landowners and Occupiers—To the Landowners of Ireland, Tenakill, Abbeyleix, April 19ᵗʰ, 1847.

I address you, gentlemen, from a great distance—the distance that separates you from the people—for I am one of the people. This is a disadvantage of some account, and might be discouraging at a season more settled. But I know that in periods of peril, when distress and disaster are present, and danger and dread are in the future, men are allowed to assume rights which must be in abeyance during ordinary times.

This is my reason and right in addressing you—that I am excited and authorised by the feelings and emergencies of the occasion. This is my claim to a hearing—not that I ask it in my own cause or, in that of the class I belong to; nor that I urge it for the sake of the masses of men who are unable to ask it for themselves; but that I claim a hearing and crave to be heard on your own behalf—on behalf of your own interest, and honour, and existence, as owners of that soil on which thousands are famishing to death for want of food.

My general object in addressing you is that of calling public notice, if I can, to the full extent of the effects which I think must inevitably follow past or present events, if the cause of these events be not checked or changed. All the facts I possess I have considered and counted in one view together, in their connection and consequence, and inferred the result.

This is a task which few others, I fear, have undertaken, nor is it any manner of surprise. Within sight and sound of this dismal calamity, amid the actual horrors of every passing hour, it is scarcely possible to look far into the future, or take thought and care for remote results. In the presence of famine men are blind to its effects.

It is doing its work in the dark, and no watch is set or warning raised. From every house and every voice throughout this land there is but one cry now—the cry for food. Food for today, and food for tomorrow—for this year and the next. But not all the clamour and outcry that has been raised throughout Ireland during the last few months has added a single pound to the supply of food, either for this year or the next.

What men were unable to do, they set about doing; what they were able to do before they left are leaving undone. For something else is wanting, and requires to be provided, besides food for today or tomorrow, else a revolution is at hand. A revolution of the worst type and character—not such as when a nation breaks up under armed violence, to reunite and rise in structure as strong as before; but such as when it falls to pieces, rotting to a final fetid ruin.

Besides the general object mentioned, I have a particular and more definite purpose, which will develop itself as I proceed. It would be useless to state it formally before it can be fully understood. Though I write more especially for you, my lords and gentlemen, landowners of Ireland, yet, I write also for the public; and shall address myself to either, as occasion may seem to demand. The failure of the potato, and consequent famine, is one of those events which come now and then to do the work of ages in a day, and change the very nature of an entire nation at once, it has even already produced a deeper social organisation than did the French Revolution—greater waste of life—wider loss of property—more than the horrors, with none of the hopes.

For its direction still seems dragging downwards, while her revolution took France to the sun—gave her wealth, and victory, and renown—a free people and a firm peasantry, lords of their own land. It has unsettled society to the foundation; deranged every interest, every class, every household.

Every man's place and relation is altered, labour has left its track, and life lost its form. One entire class, the most numerous and important in Ireland, has already begun to give way; and is about being displaced. The tenant-farmer of ten acres or under is being converted into an "independent labourer."

But it is accomplishing something more than mere social derangement, or a dislocation of classes. It has come, as if commissioned, to produce at length, and not too soon, a dissolution of that state and order of existence in which we have heretofore been living. The constitution of society that has prevailed in this island can no longer maintain itself, or be maintained.

It has been tried for generations; it has now, at least, been fully and finally tested; and the test has proved fatal. It was ever unsound and infirm, and is now breaking to pieces under the first severe experiment, an experiment which that of any other country would have easily withstood.

Nor heaven nor human nature will suffer it to be re-established or continue. If the earth, indeed, with all things therein, was made wholly for the few, and none of it for the many, then may it continue;

and if all creation was made for you, my lords and gentlemen, and none for us, then it may continue; if men are bound to live on for ever, slaves to a dominion that dooms them to toil, and cold, and hunger—to hardship and suffering in every shape; if they have no right even to life except at another's license, then may it continue; if they be bound to submit in patience to perish of famine and famine-fever, then it may continue.

But if all have a right to live in freedom and comfort on their own labour; if the humblest among them has a claim to full, secure and honest subsistence, not the knavish and beggarly subsistence of the poorhouse, then that constitution cannot and it shall not be re-established again.

When society fails to perform its duty and fulfil its office of providing for its people, it must take another and more effective form, or it must cease to exist. When its members begin to die out under destitution—when they begin to perish in thousands under famine and the effects of famine—when they begin to desert and fly from the land in hundreds of thousands under the force and fear of deadly famine—then it is time to see it is God's will that society should stand dissolved, and assume another shape and action, and He works His will by human hands and natural agencies.

The case has arisen even now in Ireland, and the effect has already followed in part. Society stands dissolved. In effect, as well as of right, it stands dissolved, and another requires to be constituted. To the past we can never return, even if we would. The potato was our sole and only capital, to live and work on, to make much or little of; and on it the entire social economy of this country was founded, formed and supported.

That system and state of things can never again be resumed or restored; not even should the potato return. A new adjustment is now to be formed, is to form and develop itself; a new social order to be arranged; a new people to be organised. Or otherwise, that people itself is about to become extinct. Either of these is inevitable, and either is desirable. In condition, and character, and conduct, a stain to earth, a scandal and a shame among the nations, a grievance to Heaven, this people has been for ages past a dark spot in the path of the sun.

Nature and Heaven can bear it no longer. To any one who either looks to an immediate directing Providence, or trusts to a settle course of natural causes, it is clear that this island is about to take existence under a new tenure, or else that Nature has issued her decree, often issued heretofore, against nations and races, and even for the same crime—that one other imbecile and cowardly people shall cease to exist, and no longer cumber the earth.

The power of framing a new order is in your hands, my lords and gentlemen, if you choose to exercise it. The work of reconstruction belongs of right to you, if you have the wisdom and the will to do it. It is in emergencies and occasions like the present, rather than in ordinary and settled times, that a national aristocracy is required, and if they be not worthy of such occasions they are worthless altogether.

It is a time like this that tries and tests the worth of a class, as it tests the worth of individual men. Not to time should the task be committed, nor to chance; not to the government of England, which is incompetent to the case; not to the parliament of England, where you are made a mark for pelting at; nor to the desperate remedies of men whom you have, yourselves, made desperate.

Ireland demands from you now something more than her present dole of daily food—a mode and system of providing full food for herself. She looks to you for this—that she be not condemned to live as a beggar on public alms, nor as a pauper on public works and poorhouse rations; but aided or enabled to find or form a mode of making her bread in all future time by free, unforced and honest labour.

She has lost her means of living; she requires some other, more sufficient and secure than those she has lost. Her demand, in full and fine, is for what is of more effective worth and weight than all the political constitutions that were ever promised—for what senates or sovereigns cannot make or unmake, but men must make for themselves—her demand for a new SOCIAL CONSTITUTION, under which to live.

This is the task you are called on to undertake, the work you are wanted to do, or forfeit your footing in this island of ours—a work to which political constitution is light in comparison and little in importance. Political rights are but paper and parchment. It is the social constitution that determines the condition and character of a people—that makes and moulds the life of man.

We are now living in the midst of a social anarchy, in which no man knows with certainty what he is, or what he can call his own. Never was government or guidance more necessary to a people; but government or guidance there is none, for the great purpose needed. An extreme and extraordinary case has arisen—one that seldom arises in modern times—and not to be judged or treated by any ordinary law.

A new structure of society has to be created; and the country has a right to require of you to counsel and conduct and lead her; because you own her soil, because your own worth and value are in question—your interest and position involved and committed; because the work cannot so speedily and safely be done without your aid; because in some respects and in some degree you are considered specially charged with the calamitous crisis that has occurred; because your rights of ownership are thought by numbers to be the only obstacle to the creation at once of a sound system of social prosperity and happiness, which would be formed by the natural energies and social instincts of mankind, if those energies were left to act, and not fettered or interfered with by your claims of dominion; and finally, because you ought of right to be—where you have never chosen to be—at the head of the people.

And at their head or at their side you must now stand, or else your aid will not be taken. On other terms it will not now be accepted; and the work will be done by other hands than yours. You are far less important to the people than the people are to you. You cannot act or stand alone, but they can. In the case that has arisen, the main power is in their hands, and little in yours. Your power of position has departed. You cannot reform and reorganise a whole people without their own consent and co-operation. You cannot act against them—you cannot act without them. They can do what is wanted of themselves, and without your assistance.

They have the will, and may learn the way. A dissolution of the social system has taken place. The failure of the potato was the *immediate, exciting* cause. Into the *predisposing* causes it is needless for the present to inquire. There was no outrise or revolt against it. It was not broken up by violence. It was borne for ages with beggarly patience, until it perished by the irritation of God in the order of Nature.

A clear, original right returns and reverts to the people—the right of establishing and entering into a new social arrangement. The right is in them, because the power is in them. The right lodges where the power lodges. It is not a case to which governments or parliaments are competent. The sole office and duty of government under the circumstances is that of supporting the destitute, and maintaining the public order during the period of transition and reorganisation.

Should it attempt doing more than this, it will be assuming a power which it does not possess, and cannot even make an effort to exercise without committing injustice, doing injury and suffering defeat. With the great body and mass of the people, in their original character and capacity, resides, of necessity, the power, in its full plenitude, of framing or falling into a new form of organisation—a new mode of living and labour.

Your aid, my lords and gentlemen, is most desirable, if accorded on terms and in a mode which would be thought likely to contribute to general benefit and happiness. On other terms, or for other objects—with a view to your own personal interests alone, and on terms to assert and secure your own position at any cost to the country and community—if offered on such views and terms, your service and aid will not be accepted; and the present condition of anarchy will be protracted by strife and struggle, terminating, possibly, in violent convulsion, from which you, at least, would come out the losers, whoever might be the winners.

To ensure against such a contingency, it is necessary that you should now combine and co-operate with that people from whom, for long ages, you have stood apart, aliens and enemies to them, as they to you. They count more in millions than you count in thousands. If you desire that they and you should now join hands to carry the boat over the rapids, it must be on terms which they will accept; on terms of advantage to them as well as to you—and the first condition and very basis of a union must be the distinct acknowledgement and assertion, in its widest extent, in its fullest force, power, and plenitude, of the principle of ALLEGIANCE TO COUNTRY.

On any other basis, no federation can form or be formed, take effect, or be of force, in Ireland now. To save mistake I ought to mention, and mark what is I do not mean, as well as what my meaning is. I do not mean that you should declare for Repeal. I scarcely know that I can call myself a Repealer, further than this—I would not say aye to the question if were put to me to decide.

The results of Repeal would depend on the means and men by whom it should have been accomplished. It might give to Ireland all that Ireland wants, and is withering in want of—equal liberty and equal laws, science and art, manufacture and trade, respect and renown; wealth to the merchant, security and comfort to the cottage; its pride of power and place to the castle, fame and fortune to genius and talent, all of that which ennobles and endears to man the land he lives in—this it might do.

It might subject us to an odious and ignoble tyranny. I am far from wishing you to take any course that would pledge you to Repeal, or to any other political measure. I do not write with a view to Repeal, or any other political object whatever. My meaning is far more general, and states itself in more general terms.

Nothing is requisite or required that would commit you to particulars, to any political party, cause, or course of conduct. But a full act and avowal of attachment and allegiance to this island, in priority and preference to any and every other country—this is required, and will be strictly required; not in mere idle form of protest and profession, but in full efficient proof and practice that Ireland is your own mother-country, and her people your people,— that her interest and honour, her gain and her glory, are counted as your own,—that her rights and liberties you will defend, as part of your inheritance,—that in peace you will lead her progress, and carry her banner in battle,—that your labour shall be in her service, and your lives laid down at her need,—that henceforth you will be, not a foreign garrison but a national guard,—this you must declare and adopt, as the principle of your proceeding, and the spirit of your action, and the rule of your order; for these are the duties of nobility.

Adopt this principle, and you are armed; on it is your safety and your strength; the future is fettered at your feet; and your name and race shall flourish and not fail. Ireland is yours for ages, on the condition that you will be Irishmen in name, in faith, in fact. Refuse it, and you commit yourselves, in the position of paupers, to the mercy of English ministers and English members; you throw your very existence on English support, which England soon may find too costly to afford; you lie at the feet of events, you lie in the way of a people, and the movement of events and the march of a people shall be over you.

Allegiance to this fair island; it is your title of tenure to the lands you hold, and in right of it you hold them. If you deny and disown it, you assert another title, and must determine to hold your inheritance by force, at your own will and to our injury, in despite and defiance for ours forever.

This would be a bootless and feeble insult, and dangerous withal; for your tittle is worth little indeed under the law you would appeal to: that while from Ireland you take rank and revenue, blood and birth and name—everything that makes home, and binds to country—yet you look not to her, but to another land, for home and country; that you desert and disown, if not hate her old native people; that in England are your hearts and hopes, and that all your household gods are English.

This crime is charged to you; unjustly charged, I trust it is—for a worse crime, and more infamous than disloyalty to kings or crowns, is disloyalty or treason to country. It is a crime not made by lawyers, but made by God; a crime against Nature itself—against all its laws, affections, interests and instincts. Yet the charge is not made against you without colour of truth and show of reason.

On every question that arises, in every contest and collision, whether of honour or interest, you take side and cause with England. All blame for this does not rest on you; but some of it does. Much and most of it rests on a class of men whose claim to attention, however strong, I must defer to a future letter. All such ground of charge must be removed and renounced.

For ever, henceforth, the owners of our soil must be Irish. To all who own land or living in Ireland, Ireland must henceforth be the Queen-island. She holds in her hands the hostages for their fealty, and will not longer put up with TREASON. On no other common ground or general principle can a federation take place between the nobles of the land and the nation at large, than that of common faith and fealty to this their common country.

The formation of the Irish Party was hailed at the time by many as one step of a movement in the direction of Ireland. It may, perhaps, indicate a change of ideas, if not of feelings. You have probably begun to find out that if your feelings are English, yet your fortunes are Irish; that Ireland's peril is perilous to yourselves; that in renouncing your country, and adopting another, you renounce and revolt from the laws of Nature; and that Nature itself is strong enough to punish the treason.

You have, moreover, got some slight cause to doubt whether England esteems your attachment as of any value, your interest as of much importance, or your very existence as worth the expense and trouble of supporting. But we recognise nothing Irish in this party except its name; nothing that can entitle it to command or call round it the hearts or hopes of this people; or raise it to any higher position than that of a mere club, and a petty club, formed by a class for the single object of saving its own little interests from injury, at any cost to the country.

Whether for its professed or private objects, whether as an Irish party or as a landowner's club, it is equally and utterly inefficient, and can do nothing for the salvation of the country or for yours. It excludes the people. It embraces no great public principles, passions, purpose, or policy. It bears no banner, and shows no motto. It rallies no support and inspires no confidence; proposes nothing, and promises nothing.

To resist the minister, should his measures of relief or improvement be deemed injurious to the landowners,—this appears the sole object of the Irish Party. But your claims as landowners are no longer maintainable or defensible on their own merits and means. To maintain, you must connect them with those of your country.

A union between parties of the same class—a union of landowners with each other—is adequate to no purpose now. The union required is a union between all classes of whom the people is composed. You are powerless without a people beside or behind you. You must call the commons into your council; and make their private interests and public objects—nay, even perhaps their public passions—a part of your policy. The Irish Party must expand and enlarge into the Irish people; or another and more effective association be framed.

To organise a new mode and condition of labour—a new industrial system; to frame and fix a new order of society; in a word, to give to Ireland a new Constitution, under which the natural capacity of this country would be put into effective action; the resources of its land, labour and capital developed and made available; its slumbering and decaying energies of mind and muscle excited, directed and employed, and the condition and character of its people reconstructed, improved and elevated; this, I have already stated, is the general object which now calls for the united action of the landowners and the people of Ireland in association assembled.

The energies of nature and action of time working together in their wonted course and current will, indeed, in long or short, be adequate, without aid or effort of ours, to form a new and effective settlement of society; but the fabric thus formed will be raised out of the relics and rest on the ruins, of the present existing people in all its classes.

For their own safety and preservation, it is necessary that all those classes should now combine to take the direction of that resolution which will otherwise effect itself, and which, indeed, is in actual process of being effected, without their consent, control, or guidance. That position has become too perilous to maintain.

Your path of safety, as well as of honour, is now the public highway. No byways of your own will carry you through the perils that beset, and the greater perils that are before you. There are many and important questions at issue between you and the landholders, between you and the labourers, between you and the people at large, between you and other classes of the people, between those classes among themselves.

No government, no legislation, no general statutes, no special statutes, no power on earth but the parties concerned; no mode on earth save that of voluntary agreement, can settle those questions. Why should we not meet and settle them amicably? Leave them not to be settled by time or to be settled by strength.

What! To create a complete and efficient industrial economy; to form and give force to a new state and mode of existence; to organise and animate and put into healthy and vigorous action that complex living machine, a social system; to frame and adjust the fabric of society—its mightiest proportions and minutest parts, with all its vast and various interests, arrangements, orders and conditions, independent yet involved, conflicting yet co-operating; what! To do all this?

A work impossible to man; and which, in extent or detail, he never yet undertook or attempted to perform. A work of which the theory and principles are beyond his knowledge or discovery, and the practical execution beyond his utmost power. Nature has reserved it to herself, to effect by a process of her own; for which no artificial process ever was or can be substituted with success. A work we cannot do; God's hand alone, not man's, can do it. True—and neither can you form in all its parts the smallest plant that grows. But sow the seed and the plant forms. The powers of vitality require but to be set in movement, and the contrivances of Nature left free to act.

Even so it is in the case we consider. That work may be done, and *you* must do it or others will; and you must do it at once, for it cannot be waited for. Nor is it, when examined, an undertaking that need dazzle or daunt by its magnitude or multiplicity the meanest mind of all among us. It includes no such complication of difficult questions as it may seem to do; and the only question actually involved is on easy of settlement when put in comparison with its apparent mass.

Its theory contains itself in a single principle; its practical solution is comprised and completed in a single operation. Lay but the foundation and the work is done. Lay the foundation, Nature effects the rest; society forms and fits itself—even as the plant grows when the seed is sown.

Lay deep and strong, the only foundation that is firm under the foot of a nation—a secure and independent agricultural peasantry. A secure and independent agricultural peasantry is the only base on which a people ever rises or can be raised, or on which a nation can safely rest. A productive and prosperous husbandry is the sole groundwork of a solid social economy.

On it and out of it springs the mechanic, and artisan, and trading dealer; fed and fostered by it these swell into the manufacturer and merchant, who multiply into merchants and manufacturers; sustained by it still these enlarge, and gather, and solidify into companies, corporations, classes—into great manufacturing and mercantile systems and interests, which often, like unnatural children, disown and desert the mother that bore and the nurse that fed them; without it there is neither manufacturer, nor trade, nor means to make them, for it is agriculture alone that furnishes these means. Food is our first want—to procure it our first work.

The agricultural class, therefore, must precede and provide for every other. It is first in order of nature, necessity, and time. It is an abundant agriculture alone that creates and sustains manufactures, and arts, and traffic. It is an increasing agriculture alone that extends them. For it is the surplus of food it accumulates, after providing ordinary subsistence, that forms new wants and demands, and the modes and means to meet and satisfy them.

Such is the actual process, a process that never yet was reversed, or carried out in any other course or order; so it was at first, and so it will be forever—in every time, in every clime, in every country. Adopt this process; create what has never yet existed in Ireland, an active and efficient husbandry, a secure and independent agricultural peasantry, able to accumulate as well as to produce; do this, and you raise a thriving and happy community, a solid social economy, a prosperous people, an effective nation.

Create the husbandman and you create the mechanic, the artisan, the manufacturer and merchant. Thus you will work out the ordinance of God, in the order and with the powers of nature. All the natural motives and means with which man is endowed will come then to your relief and assistance, and do the rest.

Any further interference with the course and process of natural laws would be useless and mischievous. Neither monarchs nor mobs ever yet were able to manage or modify that natural process, or ever attempted to enforce interference without doing grievous injury and gross injustice. The abortive and mischievous legislation of both old and recent times affords lessons enough of this, if we choose to learn them.

There seems to be a vague impression on a large portion of the public mind of this country that national attention and exertion, as well as individual effort, should be directed into a course the reverse in its steps and stages of that rational order I have pointed out. We are in the habit of hearing it asserted that a large development of manufacturing industry is what Ireland needs, and that to establish it should be her chief object.

It is even assumed, not unfrequently, that a manufacturing system must precede, and is the only means of promoting, the improvement and prosperity of agriculture itself. This is an error I would wish to see abandoned. It distracts effort and attention from the point on which both ought to be directed, and on which they could act with effect.

I am prepared to prove—what, indeed, any man may prove to himself—that neither by the private enterprise of individuals or companies, neither by the force of national feeling anywhere exerted, neither by public association or public action of any kind or extent, nor by Government aid, if such aid could be expected—neither by these or any other means and appliances can a manufacturing system be established in Ireland, nor so much as a factory built on firm ground, until the support of a numerous and efficient agricultural yeomanry be first secured!

Good friends! You that are recommending us to encourage native manufacture and to form manufacturing associations; tradesmen and townsmen of Ireland! Will you cease to follow a phantom, and give hand and help to create such a yeomanry?

My general object, the formation of a new social economy, thus resolves itself into the formation of a new agricultural system. The principles on which that new system is to be founded must either be settled by agreement between the landowners and the people, or they must be settled by a struggle. What I think those principles ought to be, if they be made articles of agreement, as well as the practical mode of arriving at and arranging such agreement, I shall take another opportunity of stating.

You, however, my lords and gentlemen, it would appear from your present proceedings, have already settled among yourselves the entire future economy of your country—determined the fortunes and fate of this entire island—disposed of the existence of this little people of eight millions. The small land-holdings are to be "consolidated" into large farms, the small landowners "converted" into "independent labourers"; those labourers are, of course, to be paupers—those paupers to be supported by a poor law—that poor law is to be in your hands to manage and administer.

Thus is to be got rid of the surplus of population beyond what the landowners require. Meantime, by forcible ejectments, forced surrender, and forced emigration, you are effecting the process of "conversion" a *little* too rapidly, perhaps, for steady and safe working.

And so, it seems, you have doomed a people to extinction? And decreed to abolish Ireland? The undertaking is a large one. Are you sure your strength will bear you through it? Or are you sure your strength will not be tested? The settlement you have made requires nothing to give it efficacy, except the assent or acquiescence of eight millions of people. Will they assent or acquiesce?

Will Ireland, at last, perish like a lamb, and let her blood sink in the ground, or will she turn as turns the baited lion? For my own part I can pronounce no opinion, and for you, my lords and gentlemen, if you have any doubts on the question, I think it would be wisdom to pause in your present course of proceeding until steps can be taken and measures adopted for effecting an accommodation and arrangement between you and the present occupiers of the soil, on terms that would preserve the rights and promote the interests of each party.

If you persevere in enforcing a clearance of your lands you will force men to weigh your existence, as landowners, against the existence of the Irish people. The result of the struggle which that question might produce ought, at best, to be a matter of doubt in your minds; even though you should be aided, as you doubtless would be, by the unanimous and cordial support of the people of England, whose respect and esteem for you are so well known and loudly attested.

I have the honour to remain, my lords and gentlemen, your humble and obedient servant,

JAMES F. LALOR.

home Rule

H ome Rule was the proposed self-government of Ireland within the United Kingdom rather than outright independence. The Home Rule movement originated in the 1870s as Irish nationalism began to shift its energy toward parliamentary reform. it began with Isaac Butt's founding of the Home Government Association in 1870, but it gained significant traction when it came under the leadership of the younger and more dynamic Charles Stewart Parnell. Parnell became the central figure in Irish politics after taking the helm of the Home Rule League – reformed by Parnell into the Irish Parliamentary Party in 1882. Parnell's tactful advocacy and skilled use of parliamentary procedure brought Ireland's demand for self-governance to the forefront of British politics in a period when Parnell's party held the balance of power in the House of Commons, most notably with the First Home Rule Bill in 1886.

Born into a Protestant landowning family in County Wicklow, Parnell was a charismatic and enigmatic figure who won the admiration of all who encountered him, including his political opposition. The British Prime Minister William Gladstone, who Parnell converted to supporting Home Rule, described Parnell as "the most remarkable man I ever met. I do not say the ablest man; I say the most remarkable and the most interesting. He was an intellectual phenomenon."

Parnell's influence extended beyond Britain when, in 1880, he addressed the U.S. Congress, passionately advocating for Irish self-governance and rallying American support, which bolstered the movement's international profile. Parnell's strategy of appealing to the sympathies of Irish-America would later become central to the strategy of Sinn Féin during the Irish War of Independence. Parnell's leadership in the Home Rule period gave the Irish a strong sense of independence that would plant the seeds for the future nationalist revolution. His "Cork Address," delivered in 1885, stands out as a particularly powerful expression of his leadership.

In the address, Parnell outlines the goal of his party to restore "Grattan's Parliament", referring to the Constitution of 1782 which granted the Kingdom of Ireland a substantial degree of autonomy from Great Britain. This autonomy was abolished by the Acts of Union passed in response to the 1798 Rebellion, and Ireland was fully absorbed into the United Kingdom by 1801.

Although Parnell notes that his party "cannot under the British constitution ask for more than the restitution" of Grattan's Parliament, he emphasises that he views this as a stepping stone to a greater sovereignty for Ireland. It's a practical yet passionate plea, reflecting Parnell's tact in balancing the nationalist demands of his countrymen with navigating parliamentary politics.

Though Parnell died young (in 1891, at age just 45) his influence loomed large over the next generation of nationalists. Three decades later, Pearse would summon Parnell's pale and angry ghost alongside Tone, Davis, Lalor, and Mitchel, to condemn the failure of his successors. Despite his short life and a political career that ended in scandal – Parnell became politically isolated and watched his party split after the revelation of his adulterous affair with a woman named Kitty O'Shea – Parnell's influence endured because he was, in Pearse's words, "less a political thinker than an embodied conviction; a flame that seared, a sword that stabbed."

Address to the United States Congress

Charles Stewart Parnell

February 2nd, 1880.

Mr. Chairman and Gentlemen of the House of Representatives, I have to thank you for the honour that you have conferred upon me in permitting me to address this august assembly upon the state of affairs in my unhappy country. The public opinion of the people of America will be of the utmost importance in enabling us to obtain a just and suitable settlement of the Irish question. I have seen, since I have been in this country, so many tokens of the good wishes of the American people towards Ireland I feel at a loss to express my sense of the enormous advantage and service which is daily being done to the cause of my country in this way. We do not seek to embroil your Government with the Government of England, but we claim that the public opinion and sentiment of a free country like America is entitled to find expression wherever it is seen that the laws of freedom are not observed.

Mr. Speaker and gentlemen, the most pressing question in Ireland is, at the present moment, the tenure of land. That question is a very old one. It dates from the first settlement of Ireland from England. The struggle between those who owned the land on the one side and those who tilled it on the other has been a constant one, and up to the present moment, scarcely any ray of light has ever been let in upon the hard fate of the tillers of the soil in that country. But many of us, who are observing now the course of events, believe that the time is fast approaching when the artificial and cruel system of land tenure prevailing in Ireland is bound to fall and to be replaced by a more natural and more just one. I could quote many authorities to show you what this system is. The feudal tenure has been tried in many countries. and it has been found wanting everywhere, but in no country has it wrought so much destruction and proved so pernicious as in Ireland. We have, as the result of that feudal tenure, constant and chronic poverty. We have our people discontented and hopeless. Even in the best years the state of the people is one of constant poverty, and when, as on the present occasion, the crops fail and a bad year comes round, we see terrific famines sweeping across the face of our land and claiming their victims in hundreds of thousands. Mr. Froude, the distinguished English historian, gives his testimony with regard to this land system in the following words:

"But of all the fatal gifts which we bestowed upon our unhappy possession was the English system of owning land. Land, properly speaking, cannot be owned by anyone. It belongs to all the human race. Laws have to be made to secure the profits of their industry to those who cultivate it; but the private property of this or that person, which he is entitled to deal with as he pleases, land ought never to be, and never, strictly speaking, is. In Ireland, as in all primitive associations, the laud was divided amongst the tribes. Each tribe owned its own district. Under the feudal system the property was held by the Crown, as representing the nation, while the subordinate tenures were held with duties attached to them and were liable, on non-fulfillment, to forfeiture."

Now, I look upon this testimony of Mr. Froude's as a most important and valuable one, coming, as it does, from an English source and a source which cannot be called prejudiced in favour of Ireland. As Mr. Froude says, property has its duties under the feudal system of tenure as well as its rights, but in Ireland those enjoying the monopoly of the land have only considered that they had rights, and have always been forgetful of their duties, so that, bad as this feudal tenure must be, it has worked in a way to intensify its evil tenfold. I find that a little further on Mr. Froude again speaks to the following effect:

"If we had been more faithful in our stewardship Ireland would have been as wealthy and prosperous as the sister island, and not at the mercy of a potato blight. We did what we could. We subscribed money. We laid a poor law upon the land, but all to no purpose. The emigrants went away with rage in their hearts and a longing hope of revenge hereafter with America's help."

I could multiply the testimony of distinguished sources and distinguished men to the same effect, but I shall content myself with quoting from one more, Professor Blackie, the professor of Greek in Edinburgh University, who, in the 'Contemporary Review' of this month, writes as follows:

"Among the many acts of baseness branding the English character in their blundering pretence of governing Ireland, not the least was the practice of confiscating the laud, which by real law, belonged to the people, and giving it, not to honest, resident cultivators which might have been a polite sort of theft, but to cliques of greedy and grasping oligarchs who did nothing for the country they had appropriated but suck its blood in the name of land rent and squander its wealth under the name of fashion and pleasure in London."

Now, we have been told by the landlord party as their defence of the system, that the true cause of Irish poverty and Irish discontent is the crowded state of that country, and I admit to the fullest extent that there are portions of Ireland which are too crowded. The barren lands of the West of Ireland, whither the people were driven from the fertile lands after the famine, are too crowded, but the fertile portions of Ireland maintain scarcely any population at all, and remain as vast hunting grounds for the pleasure of the landlord class. Before, then, we talk of emigration as the cure for all the ills of Ireland, I should like to see the rich plains of Meath, Kildare, and Tipperary, instead of being the desert wastes they are to-day, supporting the teeming and prosperous population that they are so capable of maintaining. You may drive at the present moment for ten or twenty miles through these great and rich counties without meeting a human being or seeing a single house, and it is a remarkable testimony to the horrible way in which the land system has been administered in Ireland that the fertile country had proved the destruction of the population, instead of being their support.

Only on the poor lands have our people been allowed to settle, and there these are crowded in numbers far too great for the soil to support. I should like to see the next emigration from the west to the east, instead of from the east to the west—from the barren hills of Connemara back to the fertile plains of Meath, and when the resources of my country have been fully taken advantage of and fully developed, when the agricultural prosperity of Ireland been secured, then, if we have any surplus population, we shall cheerfully give it to this great country. Then our emigrants will go willingly and as free men, not shovelled out by a forced emigration, a disgrace to the country that they came from and to humanity in general. Then our emigrants would come to you as come the Germans, with money in their pockets, education to enable them to push out to your Western lands instead of hanging about the Eastern cities, doomed to hard manual labour, and many of them falling a prey to the worst evils of modern city civilization.

I have noticed within the last few days a very remarkable testimony to this question of overcrowding in one of the newspapers of this country, the American "Nation," a journal, I believe, distinguished in the walks of literature, and whose opinion is entitled to every weight and consideration. The "Nation" says that the remedy for Irish poverty is to be found io the great multiplication of peasant properties, and not by emigration as many suppose. There is little question that emigration is good for those who emigrate, but it leaves gaps in the home population which are soon filled up by a fresh poverty-stricken mass.

A writer in the London "Times," giving an account of the island of Guernsey, shows that it supports in marvellous prosperity a population of 30,000 on the area of 10,000 acres, while Ireland has a cultivable area of 15,500,000 acres, and would, if as densely peopled as Guernsey, support a population of 45,000,000, instead of only 5,000,000 as at present. The climate of Guernsey, too, is as moist as that of Ireland, and the island is hardly any nearer to the great markets, but nearly every man in it owns his own farm, and the law facilitates his getting a farm in fee on easy terms.

Now, Mr. Speaker, and gentlemen of the House of Representatives, the remedy that we propose for the state of affairs in Ireland is an alteration of the land tenure prevailing there. We propose to imitate the example of Prussia and of other Continental countries where the feudal tenure has been tried, found wanting, and abandoned; and we also propose to make or give an opportunity to every tenant occupying a farm in Ireland to become the owner of his own farm.

This may perhaps seem at first sight a startling proposition, and I shall be told about the rights of property and vested interests and individual ownership, but we have the high authority of Mr. Froude, the English historian, which I have just quoted to you, that land, properly speaking, cannot be owned by any man. "It belongs to all the human race. Laws have to be made to secure the profits of their industry to those who cultivate it, but the private property of this or of that person, which he is entitled to deal with as he pleases, land ought never to be, and never, strictly speaking, is." We say that if it can be proved, as it has been abundantly proved, that terrible suffering and constant poverty are inflicted upon millions of the population of Ireland, then we may reasonably require from the Legislature that, paying due regard to vested interests and giving them fair compensation, they should terminate the system of ownership of the soil by the few in Ireland and replace it by one giving the ownership of the soil to the many. We have, as I pointed out, historical precedents for that course.

The King of Prussia, in 1811, by Royal Edict, seeing the evils of the feudal tenure, transferred all the land of his country from the nobles to the tenants. He compensated the nobles by giving them bonds bearing four per cent interest, and he ordained that the tenants should repay to the State the principal of these bonds by annual instalments of five per cent, extending over a term of years. The preamble to this edict is so very remarkable that I would venture to trespass upon your time for a moment to read it, if you would permit it:

"We, Frederic William, by the grace of God King of Prussia, having convinced ourselves both by personal experience in oar own domains and by that of many of lords of manors of the great advantages which have occurred both to the lord and the peasant by the transformation of peasant holdings into proprietary by the commutation of the rents on the basis of a fair indemnity, and having consulted in regard to this weighty matter experienced farmers, ordain and decree as follows: — That all tenants of hereditary holding, whatever the size of the holding, shall, by the present edict, become proprietary holding after paying the landlords the indemnity fixed by the Act."

But we have also precedents afforded by the Legislature of Great Britain for this course. The Legislature of Great Britain has already, under the Bright clauses of the Land Act, expressed its approval of the principle that a class of peasant owners should he created in Ireland. That Act permitted the State to advance to the tenants desiring to purchase their holdings two-thirds of the purchase money. This two-thirds was to be repaid by instalments of five per cent, extending over thirty-five years. Those clauses have remained, for a variety of reasons which I could not venture to trespass on your time long enough to explain, up to the present time a dead letter, but I see that Mr. John Bright, the eminent Reformer, one of the originators and fellow-labourers with Cobden in the repeal of the Corn Laws, now comes forward and proposes to amend these clauses very considerably, so as to make them more workable. In a cable from London I find that, speaking at Birmingham the other day, Mr. Bright proposes to appoint a Government commission to go to Dublin with power to sell land of landlords to tenants wishing to buy and advance them three-fourths of the purchase money, principal and interest to be repaid in thirty-five years.

Such a measure, Mr. Bright believed, would meet the desire of the Irish people. The commission should assist the tenant to purchase whenever the landlord was willing to sell. He recommended compulsory sale only where the land was owned by London companies, as in the case of large tracts near Londonderry. He expressed the belief that self-interest and the force of public opinion would soon compel the landlords to sell to the tenants. Now this proposal is undoubtedly a very great reform and an immense advance upon the present state of affairs, and while we could not accept it as a final settlement of the land question, yet we should gladly welcome it as an advance in our direction and be willing to give it a fair trial.

The radical difference between our proposition and that of Mr. Bright is that we think that the State should adopt the system of compulsory expropriation of the land, whereas Mr. Bright thinks that it may be left to self-interest and the force of public opinion to compel the landlord to sell—that is the word he uses "compel." While I agree with Mr. Bright in thinking that in all probability, if his proposal were adopted, the present land agitation in Ireland, if maintained at its present vigour, would compel the landlords to sell to the tenants at fair rents. I ask the House of Representatives of America what would they think of statesmen who, while acknowledging the justness of our principle that the tenants in Ireland ought to own the land, shrinks, at the same time, from asking the Legislature of his country to sanction that principle, and leaves to an agitation, such as is now going on in Ireland, the duty of enforcing that which the Parliament of Great Britain should enforce.

I think you will agree with me that this attempt on the part of the British Parliament to transfer its obligations and its duties to the hopeless, starving peasantry of Connemara is neither a dignified nor a worthy one, and the sooner our Parliament comes to recognise its duties in this respect the better it will be for all parties and the Government of Great Britain. Mr. Speaker and gentlemen, I have to apologise for having trespassed upon your attention at such great length, and to give you my renewed and heartiest thanks for the very great attention and kindness with which you have listened to my feeble and imperfect utterances in reference to this question. I regret that this cause has not been pleaded by an able man, but at least the cause is good, and although put before you imperfectly, it is so strong and so just that it cannot fail in obtaining recognition at your hands and at the hands of the people of this country.

It will be a proud boast for America if, after having obtained, secured, and ratified her own freedom by sacrifices unexampled in the history of any nation she were now, by the force of her public opinion, alone, by the respect with which all countries look upon any sentiment prevailing in America—if she were now to obtain for Ireland, without the shedding of one drop of blood, without drawing the sword, without one threatening message, the solution of this great question.

For my part, I, as one who boasts of American blood feeling proud in the importance which has been universally attached on all sides to American opinion with regard to this matter, I feel proud in saying and believing that the time is very near at hand when you have, in the way I have mentioned, and in no other way, been a most important factor in bringing about a solution of the Irish land question.

And then, Mr. Speaker and gentlemen, those Irish famines, now so periodical, which compel us to appear as beggars and mendicants before the world—a humiliating position to any man, but a still more humiliating for a proud nation like ours—these Irish famines will have ceased when the cause has been removed. We shall no longer be compelled to tax your magnificent generosity, and we shall be able to promise you that, with your help this shall be the last Irish famine.

CORK ADDRESS

Charles Stewart Parnell

January 21st, 1885. From the Freeman's Journal.

Mr. Mayor and ladies and gentlemen, the Mayor has kindly claimed for me your indulgence, and indeed last night when I set out upon the journey which he has described to you I felt a sinking in my heart lest when I should reach Dublin I should find myself unable to go any further, or to keep my engagement with you this evening, but when I approached Ireland I found myself getting better and better, and when I landed—when I reached Dublin, and came near your beautiful city of Cork the change became increasingly marked, so that when I reached your city I felt myself quite restored and strong, as if nothing had ever been the matter with me.

But at the same time I do intend to claim your indulgence this evening, and to make my remarks much shorter and fewer than they would have been under other circumstances. The previous speaker, Mr. Mahony, has reminded you and me that it wants a month or two of five years since the constituency of Cork honoured me by making me its representative.

My victory was a very remarkable one. Coming, as I did, amongst you, and representing the principles which I did represent, it was extraordinary that in the limited constituency of the city at that time, and with the ideas which then prevailed amongst the constituency you should have selected such a politician as me your member. Your late respected member, Joseph Ronayne, had often told me that it was impossible for Cork to return two Nationalists, and my return was the first occasion upon which two members of my way of thinking sat for and represented your city.

But great as was the advance marked by my return by a very narrow majority it was as nothing to the change which has since taken place. Altogether, leaving aside the great extension to the constituency which the Franchise Act has made, you have since shown in the election of my able colleague, Mr. Deasy, that it is no trouble for you to elect any number of Nationalists, and the present constituency of Cork under the Franchise Act will leave you in a position free from care so far as the choice of your representative goes. I do not suppose that the will of Cork will ever again be contested by the oligarchy in this city. At the election in 1880 I laid certain principles before you, and you accepted them. I said, and I pledged myself, that I should form one of an independent Irish Party to act in opposition to every English Government which refused to concede the just rights of Ireland. And the longer time which is gone by since then, the more I am convinced that that is the true policy to pursue so far as Parliamentary policy is concerned, and that it will be impossible for either or both of the English parties to contend for any long time against a determined band of Irishmen acting honestly upon these principles, and backed by the Irish people. But we have not alone had that object in view—we have always been very careful not to fetter or control the people at home in any way, not to prevent them from doing anything by their own strength which it is possible for them to do. Sometimes, perhaps, in our anxiety in this direction we have asked them to do what is beyond their strength, but I hold that it is better even to encourage you to do what is beyond your strength even should you fail sometimes in the attempt than to teach you to be subservient and unreliant. You have been encouraged to organize yourselves, to depend upon the rectitude of your cause for your justification, and to depend upon the determination which has helped Irishmen through many centuries to retain the name of Ireland and to retain her nationhood. Nobody could point to any single action of ours in the House of Commons or out of it which was not based upon the knowledge that behind us existed a strong and brave people, that without the help of the people our exertions would be as nothing, and that with their help and with their confidence we should be, as I believe we shall prove to be in the near future, invincible and unconquerable. The electors—the old electors—the electors who will be swamped in the great mass of Irishmen now admitted to the rights of the Constitution so far as they existed in this country, were, on the whole, faithful to their trust. Indeed, it was not until we showed by a good many proofs that we could do without an enlargement of the franchise, and that with the old restricted suffrage we could do all that was necessary in the way of Parliamentary operations, that the opposition to the admission of the masses of the Irish people to the franchise disappeared. But I look forward to the future with a light heart. I am convinced that the five hundred or six hundred thousand Irishmen who within a year must vote for the men of their choice will be as true to Ireland, even truer to Ireland, than those who have gone before them, and that we may safely trust to them the exercise of the great and important privilege, unequalled in its greatness and its magnitude in the history of any nation, which will shortly be placed upon them. I am convinced that when the reckoning comes up after the general election of 1886 that we in Ireland shall have cause to congratulate ourselves in the possession of a strong party which will bear down all opposition, and which, aided by the organisation of our country behind us, will enable us to gain for our country those rights which were stolen from us. We shall struggle, as we have been struggling, for the great and important interests of the Irish tenant farmer. We shall ask that his industry shall not be fettered by rent. We shall ask also from the farmer in return that he shall do what in him lies to encourage the struggling manufactures of Ireland, and that he shall not think it too great a sacrifice to be called upon when he wants anything, when he has to purchase anything, to consider how he may get it of Irish material and manufacture, even suppose he has to pay a little more for it. I am sorry if the agricultural population has shown itself somewhat deficient in its sense of duty in this respect up to the present time, but I feel convinced that the matter has only to be put before them to secure the opening up of the most important markets in this country for those manufactures which have always existed, and for those which have been reopened anew, as a consequence of the recent exhibitions, the great exhibition in Dublin, and the other equally great one in Cork, which have been recently held. We shall also endeavour to secure for the labourer some recognition and some right in the land of his country. We don't care whether it be the prejudices of the farm or of the landlord that stands in his way. We consider that whatever class tries to obstruct the labourer in the possession of those fair and just rights to which he is entitled, that class should be put down, and coerced if you will, into doing justice to the labourer. We have shown our desire to benefit the labourer by the passage of the Labourers Act, which, if maimed and mutilated in many of its provisions, undoubtedly is based upon correct lines and principles which will undoubtedly do much good for that class, and undoubtedly will secure for the labouring classes a portion of what we have been striving to secure for them. Well, but gentlemen, I go back from the consideration of these questions to the land question, in which the labourers' question is also involved, and the manufacturers question. I come back, and every Irish politician must be forcibly driven back, to the consideration of the great question of National Self-Government for Ireland. I do not know how this great question will be eventually settled. I do not know whether England will be wise in time and concede to constitutional arguments and methods the restitution of that which was stolen from us towards the close of the last century. It is given to none of us to forecast the future, and just as it is impossible for us to say in what way or by what means the National question may be settled, in what way full justice may be done to Ireland, so it is impossible for us to say to what extent that justice should be done. We cannot ask for less than restitution of Grattan's Parliament, with its important privileges and wide and far-reaching constitution. We cannot under the British constitution ask for more than the restitution of Grattan's Parliament, but no man has the right to fix the boundary to the march of a nation. No man has a right to say to his country, 'Thus far shalt thou go and no further,' and we have never attempted to fix the *ne plus ultra* to the progress of Ireland's nationhood, and we never shall. But, gentlemen, while we leave those things to time, circumstances, and the future, we must each one of us resolve in our own hearts that we shall at all times do everything that within us lies to obtain for Ireland the fullest measure of her rights. In this way we shall not give up anything which the future may put in favour of our country; and while we struggle today for that which may seem possible for us with our combination, we must struggle for it with the proud consciousness that we shall not do anything to hinder or prevent better men who may come after us from gaining better things than those for which we now contend.

The Gaelic Revival

The Gaelic Revival was a cultural movement that emerged in the late 19th Century as a response to increased Anglicisation and the demise of the Irish language. The Revival aimed at rediscovering and restoring authentic Gaelic culture, including mythology, folklore, sports and language. This volume highlights two central figures of the Gaelic Revival: Michael Cusack and Douglas Hyde.

Michael Cusack, a teacher from County Clare, founded the Gaelic Athletic Association (GAA) in 1884 to revive traditional Irish sports like hurling and Gaelic football. At the time, these native Irish sports were in decline as the English sports of Rugby, Association Football and Cricket became more popular. Cusack not only viewed their decline as a loss of national identity, but he saw a revival of these martial sports as a means of strengthening community ties and restoring the fitness of the Irish race. Cusack's establishment of the GAA formalised rules for the native games and helped organise the sport nationally. This proved to be enormously successful in reversing the decline: Gaelic Football remains the dominant sport in Ireland today, with Hurling not far behind.

Douglas Hyde, a scholar and writer, approached the Revival through language and literature. Hyde co-founded the Gaelic League in 1893 to promote the use of Irish, building on his 1892 speech, "The Necessity for De-Anglicising Ireland," which called for rejecting English cultural norms. Although Hyde wanted the League to remain apolitical, the organisation attracted many nationalists. When the Irish Republic was declared with the reading of a proclamation of independence before the 1916 Rising, no less than six of the seven signatories were recognised members of Hyde's Conradh na Gaeilge. Patrick Pearse, the most well-known leader of the 1916 Rising, was the editor of the Gaelic League's newspaper An Claidheamh Soluis. While Hyde himself was disillusioned with the radical political direction the organisation was taken in, this is a testament to the great political influence the cultural revival had in reviving a sense of Irish uniqueness and independence.

Hyde's contribution to the Gaelic revival was immense: his work was largely devoted to the study and publication of traditional Irish literature and folklore, but he also contributed to the revival of interest in the language through his own poetry and essays. His work helped make the language a focal point of the Gaelic Revival, and his later uncontested selection as Ireland's first President in 1938 showed the high esteem he was held in by the former revolutionaries now in government.

A Word About Irish Athletics

Michael Cusack

From The Irishman, October 11, 1884.

No movement having for its object the social and political advancement of a nation from the tyranny of imported and enforced customs and manners can be regarded as perfect if it has not made adequate provision for the preservation and cultivation of the National pastimes of the people. Voluntary neglect of such pastimes is a sure sign of National decay and of approaching dissolution.

The strength and energy of a race are largely dependent on the National pastimes for the development of a spirit of courage and endurance. A warlike race is ever fond of games requiring skill, strength, and staying power. The best games of such a race are never free from danger. But when a race is declining in martial spirit, no matter from what cause, the national games are neglected at first and then forgotten. And as the corrupting and degrading influences first manifest themselves in capital towns and large cities, so, too, we find that the national pastimes and racial characteristics first fade and disappear from such large centres of population.

And further, as persons whose reason is unhinged often put off the substantial and decent clothes suitable to their condition, and deck themselves in gaudy frippery and fading flowers, thereby demonstrating that the throne of man's dignity is uncrowned, so, too, we find the deteriorating residents of cities and the thoughtless votaries of fashion ever impotently looking out with feverish anxiety for some change in their dreary pastimes after having abandoned those of the people. The corrupting influences which for several years have been devastating the sporting grounds of our cities and towns are fast spreading to our rural population.

Foreign and hostile laws and the pernicious influence of a hated and hitherto dominant race drove the Irish people from their trysting-places at the cross-roads and hurling fields back to their cabins where but a few years before famine and fever reigned supreme. In those wretched homes – homes consecrated by sufferings which should appal the devil – the Irish peasant too often wasted his evenings and his holidays in smoking and card-playing. A few years later a so-called revival of athletics was inaugurated in Ireland. The new movement did not originate with those who have ever had any sympathy with Ireland or the Irish people.

Accordingly labourers, tradesmen, artists, and even policemen and soldiers were excluded from the few competitions which constituted the lame and halting programme of the promoters. Two years ago every man who did not make his living either wholly or partly by athletics was allowed to compete. But with this concession came a law which is as intolerable as its existence in Ireland is degrading. The law is, that all Athletic Meetings shall be held under the rules of the Amateur Athletics Association of England, and that any person competing at any meeting not held under these rules should be ineligible to compete elsewhere.

The management of nearly all the meetings held in Ireland since has been entrusted to persons hostile to all the dearest aspirations of the Irish people. Every effort has been made to make the meetings look as English as possible – foot-races, betting, and flagrant cheating being their most prominent features. Swarms of pot-hunting mashers sprang into existence. They formed Harrier Clubs, for the purpose of training through the winter, after the fashion of English professional athletes, that they might be able to win and pawn the prizes offered for competition in the summer.

We tell the Irish people to take the management of their games into their own hands, to encourage and promote in every way every form of athletics which is peculiarly Irish, and to remove with one sweep everything foreign and iniquitous in the present system. The vast majority of the best athletes in Ireland are Nationalists. These gentlemen should take the matter in hands at once, and draft laws for the guidance of the promoters of meetings in Ireland next year. The people pay the expenses of the meetings, and the representatives of the people should have the controlling power. It is only by such an arrangement that pure Irish athletics will be revived, and that the incomparable strength and physique of our race will be preserved.

The Necessity for De-Anglicising Ireland

Douglas Hyde

Delivered before the Irish National Literary Society in Dublin, 25 November, 1892.

When we speak of "The Necessity for De-Anglicising the Irish Nation," we mean it, not as a protest against imitating what is *best* in the English people, for that would be absurd, but rather to show the folly of neglecting what is Irish, and hastening to adopt, pell-mell, and indiscriminately, everything that is English, simply because it *is* English.

This is a question which most Irishmen will naturally look at from a National point of view, but it is one which ought also to claim the sympathies of every intelligent Unionist, and which, as I know, does claim the sympathy of many.

If we take a bird's-eye view of our island to-day, and compare it with what it used to be, we must be struck by the extraordinary fact that the nation which was once, as every one admits, one of the most classically learned and cultured nations in Europe, is now one of the least so; how one of the most reading and literary peoples has become one of the *least* studious and most *un*-literary, and how the present art products of one of the quickest, most sensitive, and most artistic races on earth are now only distinguished for their hideousness.

I shall endeavour to show that this failure of the Irish people in recent times has been largely brought about by the race diverging during this century from the right path, and ceasing to be Irish without becoming English. I shall attempt to show that with the bulk of the people this change took place quite recently, much more recently than most people imagine, and is, in fact, still going on. I should also like to call attention to the illogical position of men who drop their own language to speak English, of men who translate their euphonious Irish names into English monosyllables, of men who read English books, and know nothing about Gaelic literature, nevertheless protesting as a matter of sentiment that they hate the country which at every hand's turn they rush to imitate.

I wish to show you that in Anglicising ourselves wholesale we have thrown away with a light heart the best claim which we have upon the world's recognition of us as a separate nationality. What did Mazzini say? What is Goldwin Smith never tired of declaiming? What do the *Spectator* and *Saturday Review* harp on? That we ought to be content as an integral part of the United Kingdom because we have lost the notes of nationality, our language and customs.

It has always been very curious to me how Irish sentiment sticks in this half-way house—how it continues to apparently hate the English, and at the same time continues to imitate them; how it continues to clamour for recognition as a distinct nationality, and at the same time throws away with both hands what would make it so. If Irishmen only went a little farther they would become good Englishmen in sentiment also. But—illogical as it appears—there seems not the slightest sign or probability of their taking that step. It is the curious certainty that come what may Irishmen will continue to resist English rule, even though it should be for their good, which prevents many of our nation from becoming Unionists upon the spot. It is a fact, and we must face it as a fact, that although they adopt English habits and copy England in every way, the great bulk of Irishmen and Irishwomen over the whole world are known to be filled with a dull, ever-abiding animosity against her, and—right or wrong—to grieve when she prospers, and joy when she is hurt. Such movements as Young Irelandism, Fenianism, Land Leagueism, and Parliamentary obstruction seem always to gain their sympathy and support. It is just because there appears no earthly chance of their becoming good members of the Empire that I urge that they should not remain in the anomalous position they are in, but since they absolutely refuse to become the one thing, that they become the other; cultivate what they have rejected, and build up an Irish nation on Irish lines.

But you ask, why should we wish to make Ireland more Celtic than it is—why should we de-Anglicise it at all?

I answer because the Irish race is at present in a most anomalous position, imitating England and yet apparently hating it. How can it produce anything good in literature, art, or institutions as long as it is actuated by motives so contradictory? Besides, I believe it is our Gaelic past which, though the Irish race does not recognise it just at present, is really at the bottom of the Irish heart, and prevents us becoming citizens of the Empire, as, I think, can be easily proved.

To say that Ireland has not prospered under English rule is simply a truism; all the world admits it, England does not deny it. But the English retort is ready. You have not prospered, they say, because you would not settle down contentedly, like the Scotch, and form part of the Empire. "Twenty years of good, resolute, grandfatherly government," said a well-known Englishman, will solve the Irish question. He possibly made the period too short, but let us suppose this. Let us suppose for a moment—which is impossible—that there were to arise a series of Cromwells in England for the space of one hundred years, able administrators of the Empire, careful rulers of Ireland, developing to the utmost our national resources, whilst they unremittingly stamped out every spark of national feeling, making Ireland a land of wealth and factories, whilst they extinguished every thought and every idea that was Irish, and left us, at last, after a hundred years of good government, fat, wealthy, and populous, but with all our characteristics gone, with every external that at present differentiates us from the English lost or dropped; all our Irish names of places and people turned into English names; the Irish language completely extinct; the O's and the Macs dropped; our Irish intonation changed, as far as possible by English schoolmasters into something English; our history no longer remembered or taught; the names of our rebels and martyrs blotted out; our battlefields and traditions forgotten; the fact that we were not of Saxon origin dropped out of sight and memory, and let me now put the question—How many Irishmen are there who would purchase material prosperity at such a price? It is exactly such a question as this and the answer to it that shows the difference between the English and Irish race. Nine Englishmen out of ten would jump to make the exchange, and I as firmly believe that nine Irishmen out of ten would indignantly refuse it.

And yet this awful idea of complete Anglicisation, which I have here put before you in all its crudity, is, and has been, making silent inroads upon us for nearly a century.

Its inroads have been silent, because, had the Gaelic race perceived what was being done, or had they been once warned of what was taking place in their own midst, they would, I think, never have allowed it. When the picture of complete Anglicisation is drawn for them in all its nakedness Irish sentimentality becomes suddenly a power and refuses to surrender its birthright.

What lies at the back of the sentiments of nationality with which the Irish millions seem so strongly leavened, what can prompt them to applaud such sentiments as:

"They say the British empire owes much to Irish hands,
That Irish valour fixed her flag o'er many conquered lands;
And ask if Erin takes no pride in these her gallant sons,
Her Wolseleys and her Lawrences, her Wolfes and Wellingtons.

Ah! these were of the Empire—we yield them to her fame,
And ne'er in Erin's orisons are heard their alien name;
But those for whom her heart beats high and benedictions swell,
They died upon the scaffold and they pined within the cell."

Of course it is a very composite feeling which prompts them; but I believe that what is largely behind it is the half unconscious feeling that the race which at one time held possession of more than half Europe, which established itself in Greece, and burned infant Rome, is now—almost extirpated and absorbed elsewhere—making its last stand for independence in this island of Ireland; and do what they may the race of to-day cannot wholly divest itself from the mantle of its own past. Through early Irish literature, for instance, can we best form some conception of what that race really was, which, after overthrowing and trampling on the primitive peoples of half Europe, was itself forced in turn to yield its speech, manners, and independence to the victorious eagles of Rome. We alone of the nations of Western Europe escaped the claws of those birds of prey; we alone developed ourselves naturally upon our own lines outside of and free from all Roman influence; we alone were thus able to produce an early art and literature, *our* antiquities can best throw light upon the pre-Romanised inhabitants of half Europe, and—we are our father's sons.

There is really no exaggeration in all this, although Irishmen are sometimes prone to overstating as well as to forgetting. Westwood himself declares that, were it not for Irishmen, these islands would possess no primitive works of art worth the mentioning; Jubainville asserts that early Irish literature is that which best throws light upon the manners and customs of his own ancestors the Gauls; and Zimmer, who has done so much for Celtic philology, has declared that only a spurious criticism can make an attempt to doubt about the historical character of the chief persons of our two epic cycles, that of Cuchullain and of Finn. It is useless elaborating this point; and Dr. Sigerson has already shown in his opening lecture the debt of gratitude which in many respects Europe owes to ancient Ireland. The dim consciousness of this is one of those things which are at the back of Irish national sentiment, and our business, whether we be Unionists or Nationalists, should be to make this dim consciousness an active and potent feeling, and thus increase our sense of self-respect and of honour.

What we must endeavour to never forget is this, that the Ireland of to-day is the descendant of the Ireland of the seventh century, then the school of Europe and the torch of learning. It is true that Northmen made some minor settlements in it in the ninth and tenth centuries, it is true that the Normans made extensive settlements during the succeeding centuries, but none of those broke the continuity of the social life of the island. Dane and Norman drawn to the kindly Irish breast issued forth in a generation or two fully Irishised, and more Hibernian than the Hibernians themselves, and even after the Cromwellian plantation the children of numbers of the English soldiers who settled in the south and midlands, were, after forty years' residence, and after marrying Irish wives, turned into good Irishmen, and unable to speak a word of English, while several

Gaelic poets of the last century have, like Father English, the most unmistakably English names. In two points only was the continuity of the Irishism of Ireland damaged. First, in the north-east of Ulster, where the Gaelic race was expelled and the land planted with aliens, whom our dear mother Erin, assimilative as she is, has hitherto found it difficult to absorb, and in the ownership of the land, eight-ninths of which belongs to people many of whom always lived, or live, abroad, and not half of whom Ireland can be said to have assimilated.

During all this time the continuation of Erin's national life centred, according to our way of looking at it, not so much in the Cromwellian or Williamite landholders who sat in College Green, and governed the country, as in the mass of the people whom Dean Swift considered might be entirely neglected, and looked upon as hewers of wood and drawers of water; the men who, nevertheless, constituted the real working population, and who were living on in the hopes of better days; the men who have since made America, and have within the last ten years proved what an important factor they may be in wrecking or in building the British Empire. These are the men of whom our merchants, artisans, and farmers mostly consist, and in whose hands is to-day the making or marring of an Irish nation. But, alas, *quantum mutatus ab illo*! What the battleaxe of the Dane, the sword of the Norman, the wile of the Saxon were unable to perform, we have accomplished ourselves. We have at last broken the continuity of Irish life, and just at the moment when the Celtic race is presumably about to largely recover possession of its own country, it finds itself deprived and stript of its Celtic characteristics, cut off from the past, yet scarcely in touch with the present. It has lost since the beginning of this century almost all that connected it with the era of Cuchullain and of Ossian, that connected it with the Christianisers of Europe, that connected it with Brian Boru and the heroes of Clontarf, with the O'Neills and O'Donnells, with Rory

O'More, with the Wild Geese, and even to some extent with the men of '98. It has lost all that they had—language, traditions, music, genius, and ideas. Just when we should be starting to build up anew the Irish race and the Gaelic nation—as within our own recollection Greece has been built up anew—we find ourselves despoiled of the bricks of nationality. The old bricks that lasted eighteen hundred years are destroyed; we must now set to, to bake new ones, if we can, on other ground and of other clay. Imagine for a moment the restoration of a German-speaking Greece.

The bulk of the Irish race really lived in the closest contact with the traditions of the past and the national life of nearly eighteen hundred years, until the beginning of this century. Not only so, but during the whole of the dark Penal times they produced amongst themselves a most vigorous literary development. Their schoolmasters and wealthy farmers, unwearied scribes, produced innumerable manuscripts in beautiful writing, each letter separated from another as in Greek, transcripts both of the ancient literature of their sires and of the more modern literature produced by themselves. Until the beginning of the present century there was no county, no barony, and, I may almost say, no townland which did not boast of an Irish poet, the people's representative of those ancient bards who died out with the extirpation of the great Milesian families. The literary activity of even the eighteenth century among the Gaels was very great, not in the South alone, but also in Ulster— the number of poets it produced was something astonishing. It did not, however, produce many works in Gaelic prose, but it propagated translations of many pieces from the French, Latin, Spanish, and English. Every well-to-do farmer could read and write Irish, and many of them could understand even archaic Irish. I have myself heard persons reciting the poems of Donogha More O'Daly, Abbot of Boyle, in Roscommon, who died sixty years before Chaucer was born. To this very day the people have a word for archaic Irish, which is much the same as though Chaucer's poems were handed down amongst the English peasantry, but required a special training to understand. This training, however, nearly every one of fair education during the Penal times possessed, nor did they begin to lose their Irish training and knowledge until after the establishment of Maynooth and the rise of O'Connell. These two events made an end of the Gaelicism of the Gaelic race, although a great number of poets and scribes existed even down to the forties and fifties of the present century, and a few may linger on yet in remote localities. But it may be said, roughly speaking, that the ancient Gaelic civilisation died with O'Connell, largely, I am afraid, owing to his example and his neglect of inculcating the necessity of keeping alive racial customs, language, and traditions, in which with the one notable exception of our scholarly idealist, Smith O'Brien, he has been followed until a year ago by almost every leader of the Irish race.

Thomas Davis and his brilliant band of Young Irelanders came just at the dividing of the line, and tried to give to Ireland a new literature in English to replace the literature which was just being discarded. It succeeded and it did not succeed. It was a most brilliant effort, but the old bark had been too recently stripped off the Irish tree, and the trunk could not take as it might have done to a fresh one. It was a new departure, and at first produced a violent effect. Yet in the long run it failed to properly leaven our peasantry who might, perhaps, have been reached upon other lines. I say they *might* have been reached upon other lines because it is quite certain that even well on into the beginning of this century, Irish poor scholars and schoolmasters used to gain the greatest favour and applause by reading out manuscripts in the people's houses at night, some of which manuscripts had an antiquity of a couple of hundred years or more behind them, and which, when they got illegible from age, were always recopied. The Irish peasantry at that time were all to some extent cultured men, and many of the better off ones were scholars and poets. What have we now left of all that? Scarcely a trace. Many of them read newspapers indeed, but who reads, much less recites, an epic poem, or chants an elegiac or even a hymn?

Wherever Irish throughout Ireland continued to be spoken, there the ancient MSS. continued to be read, there the epics of Cuchullain, Conor MacNessa, Déirdre, Finn, Oscar, and Ossian continued to be told, and there poetry and music held sway. Some people may think I am exaggerating in asserting that such a state of things existed down to the present century, but it is no exaggeration. I have myself spoken with men from Cavan and Tyrone who spoke excellent Irish. Carleton's stories bear witness to the prevalence of the Irish language and traditions in Ulster when he began to write. My friend Mr. Lloyd has found numbers in Antrim who spoke good Irish. And, as for Leinster, my friend Mr. Cleaver informed me that when he lived in Wicklow a man came by from the County Carlow in search of work who could not speak a word of English. Old labourers from Connacht, who used to go to reap the harvest in England and take shipping at Drogheda, told me that at that time, fifty years ago, Irish was spoken by every one round that town. I have met an old man in Wicklow, not twenty miles from Dublin, whose parents always repeated the Rosary in Irish. My friend Father O'Growny, who has done and is doing so much for the Irish language and literature at Maynooth, tells me that there, within twenty miles of Dublin, are three old people who still speak Irish. O'Curry found people within seven miles of Dublin city who had never heard English in their youth at all, except from the car-drivers of the great town. I gave an old man in the street who begged from me, a penny, only a few days ago, saying, "*Sin pighin agad*," and when he answered in Irish I asked him where he was from, and he said from *Newna* (*n' Eamhain*), *i.e.*, Navan. Last year I was in Canada and out hunting with some Red Indians, and we spent a night in the last white man's house in the last settlement on the brink of the primeval forest; and judging from a peculiarly Hibernian physiognomy that the man was Irish, I addressed him in Gaelic, and to the intense astonishment both of whites and Indians we entered into a conversation which none of them understood; and it turned out that he was from within three miles of Kilkenny, and had been forty years in that country without forgetting the language he had spoken as a child, and I, although from the centre of Connacht, understood him perfectly. When my father was a young boy in the county Leitrim, not far from Longford, he seldom heard the farm labourers and tenants speak anything but Irish amongst themselves. So much for Ulster and Leinster, but Connacht and Munster were until quite recently completely Gaelic. In fact, I may venture to say, that, up to the beginning of the present century, neither man, woman, nor child of the Gaelic race, either of high blood or low blood, existed in Ireland who did not either speak Irish or understand it. But within the last ninety years we have, with an unparalleled frivolity, deliberately thrown away our birthright and Anglicised ourselves. None of the children of those people of whom I have spoken know Irish, and the race will from henceforth be changed; for as Monsieur Jubainville says of the influence of Rome upon Gaul, England "has definitely conquered us, she has even imposed upon us her language, that is to say, the form of our thoughts during every instant of our existence." It is curious that those who most fear West Britainism have so eagerly consented to imposing upon the Irish race what, according to Jubainville, who in common with all the great scholars of the continent, seems to regret it very much, is "the form of our thoughts during every instant of our existence."

So much for the greatest stroke of all in our Anglicisation, the loss of our language. I have often heard people thank God that if the

English gave us nothing else they gave us at least their language. In this way they put a bold face upon the matter, and pretend that the Irish language is not worth knowing, and has no literature. But the Irish language *is* worth knowing, or why would the greatest philologists of Germany, France, and Italy be emulously studying it, and it *does* possess a literature, or why would a German savant have made the calculation that the books written in Irish between the eleventh and seventeenth centuries, and still extant, would fill a thousand octavo volumes.

I have no hesitation at all in saying that every Irish-feeling Irishman, who hates the reproach of West-Britonism, should set himself to encourage the efforts which are being made to keep alive our once great national tongue. The losing of it is our greatest blow, and the sorest stroke that the rapid Anglicisation of Ireland has inflicted upon us. In order to de-Anglicise ourselves we must at once arrest the decay of the language. We must bring pressure upon our politicians not to snuff it out by their tacit discouragement merely because they do not happen themselves to understand it. We must arouse some spark of patriotic inspiration among the peasantry who still use the language, and put an end to the shameful state of feeling—a thousand-tongued reproach to our leaders and statesmen—which makes young men and women blush and hang their heads when overheard speaking their own language. Maynooth has at last come splendidly to the front, and it is now incumbent upon every clerical student to attend lectures in the Irish language and history during the first three years of his course. But in order to keep the Irish language alive where it is still spoken—which is the utmost we can at present aspire to—nothing less than a house-to-house visitation and exhortation of the people themselves will do, something—though with a very different purpose—analogous to the procedure that James Stephens adopted throughout Ireland when he found her like a corpse on the dissecting table. This and some system of giving medals or badges of honour to every family who will guarantee that they have always spoken Irish amongst themselves during the year. But, unfortunately, distracted as we are and torn by contending factions, it is impossible to find either men or money to carry out this simple remedy, although to a dispassionate foreigner— to a Zeuss, Jubainville, Zimmer, Kuno Meyer, Windisch, or Ascoli, and the rest—this is of greater importance than whether Mr. Redmond or Mr. MacCarthy lead the largest wing of the Irish party for the moment, or Mr. So-and-So succeed with his election petition. To a person taking a bird's-eye view of the situation a hundred or five hundred years hence, believe me, it will also appear of greater importance than any mere temporary wrangle, but, unhappily, our countrymen cannot be brought to see this.

We can, however, insist, and we *shall* insist if Home Rule be carried, that the Irish language, which so many foreign scholars of the first calibre find so worthy of study, shall be placed on a par with—or even above—Greek, Latin, and modern languages, in all examinations held under the Irish Government. We can also insist, and we *shall* insist, that in those baronies where the children speak Irish, Irish shall be taught, and that Irish-speaking schoolmasters, petty sessions clerks, and even magistrates be appointed in Irish-speaking districts. If all this were done, it should not be very difficult, with the aid of the foremost foreign scholars, to bring about a tone of thought which would make it disgraceful for an educated Irishman—especially of the old Celtic race, MacDermotts, O'Conors, O'Sullivans, MacCarthys, O'Neills—to be ignorant of his own language—would make it at least as disgraceful as for an educated Jew to be quite ignorant of Hebrew.

We find the decay of our language faithfully reflected in the decay of our surnames. In Celtic times a great proof of the powers of assimilation which the Irish nation possessed, was the fact that so many of the great Norman and English nobles lived like the native chiefs and took Irish names. In this way the De Bourgos of Connacht became MacWilliams, of which clan again some minor branches became MacPhilpins, MacGibbons, and MacRaymonds. The Birminghams of Connacht took the name of MacFeóiris, the Stauntons became MacAveelys, the Nangles MacCostellos; the Prendergasts of Mayo became MacMaurices, the De Courcys became MacPatricks, the Bissetts of Antrim became MacEóins, and so on. Roughly speaking, it may be said that most of the English and Norman families outside of the Pale were Irish in name and manners from the beginning of the fourteenth to the middle of the seventeenth century.

In 1465 an Act was passed by the Parliament of the English Pale that all Irishmen inside the Pale should take an English name "of one towne as Sutton, Chester, Trym, Skryne, Corke, Kinsale; or colour, as white, black, brown; or art or science, as smith or carpenter; or office, as cooke, butler; and that he and his issue shall use this name" or forfeit all his goods. A great number of the lesser families complied with this typically English ordinance; but the greater ones—the MacMurroghs, O'Tooles, O'Byrnes, O'Nolans, O'Mores, O'Ryans, O'Conor Falys, O'Kellys, &c.—refused, and never did change their names. A hundred and thirty years later we find Spenser, the poet, advocating the renewal of this statute. By doing this, says Spenser, "they shall in time learne quite to forget the Irish nation. And herewithal," he says, "would I also wish the O's and Macs which the heads of septs have taken to their names to be utterly forbidden and extinguished, for that the same being an ordinance (as some say) first made by O'Brien (**Brian Borúma**) for the strengthening of the Irish, the abrogation thereof will as much enfeeble them." It was, however, only after Aughrim and the Boyne that Irish names began to be changed in great numbers, and O'Conors to become "Conyers," O'Reillys "Ridleys," O'Donnells "Daniels," O'Sullivans "Silvans," MacCarthys "Carters," and so on.

But it is the last sixty years that have made most havoc with our Milesian names. It seemed as if the people were possessed with a mania for changing them to something—anything at all, only to get rid of the Milesian sound. "Why," said O'Connell, once talking to a mass-meeting of Lord Chancellor Sugden, "you wouldn't call a decent pig Sugden." Yet he never uttered a word of remonstrance at the O'Lahiffs, O'Brollahans, and MacRorys becoming under his eyes Guthrys, Bradleys, and Rogerses. It is more than a little curious, and a very bad augury for the future independence of Ireland, that men of education and intelligence like Carleton the novelist, or Hardiman, author of the "History of Galway" and the "Irish Minstrelsy," should have changed their Milesian names, one from that of O'Cairellan, who was ancient chief of Clandermot, the other from the well-known name of O'Hargadain. In Connacht alone I know scores of Gatelys, Sextons, Baldwins, Foxes, Coxes, Footes, Greenes, Keatings, who are really O'Gatlies, O'Sesnans, O'Mulligans, O'Shanahans, MacGillacullys, O'Trehys, O'Honeens, and O'Keateys. The O'Hennesys are Harringtons, the O'Kinsellaghs, Kingsleys and Tinslys, the O'Feehillys Pickleys, and so on. O'Donovan, writing in 1862, gives a list of names which had recently been changed in the neighbourhood of Cootehill, Co. Cavan. These Irish names of MacNebo, MacIntyre, MacGilroy, MacTernan, MacCorry, MacOscar, MacBrehon, O'Clery, Murtagh, O'Drum, &c., were becoming, or had become, Victory, Victoria, Callwell, Freeman, King, Nugent, Gilman, Leonard, Godwin, Goodwin, Smyth, Golderich, Golding, Masterton, Lind, Crosby, Grosby, Crosse, Corry, Cosgrove, Judge, Brabacy, Brabazon, Clarke, Clerkin,

Cunningham, Drummond, Tackit, Sexton, and Mortimer—not a bad attempt at West-Britonising for one little town!

Numbers of people, again, like Mr. Davitt or Mr. Hennessy, drop the O and Mac which properly belong to their names; others, without actually changing them, metamorphose their names, as we have seen, into every possible form. I was told in America that the first Chauncey who ever came out there was an O'Shaughnessy, who went to, I think, Maryland, in the middle of the last century, and who had twelve sons, who called themselves Chauncey, and from whom most of or all the Chaunceys in America are descended. I know people who have translated their names within the last ten years. This vile habit is going on with almost unabated vigour, and nobody has ever raised a protest against it. Out of the many hundreds of O'Byrnes— offshoots of the great Wicklow chieftains—in the city of New York, only four have retained that name; all the rest have taken the Scotch name of Burns. I have this information from two of the remaining four, both friends of my own, and both splendid Gaelic scholars, though from opposite ends of Ireland, Donegal and Waterford. Of two brothers of whom I was lately told, though I do not know them personally, one is an O'Gara, and still condescends to remain connected with the patron of the Four Masters and a thousand years of a glorious past, whilst the other (through some etymological confusion with the word Caraim, which means "I love") calls himself Mr. Love! Another brother remains a Brehony, thus showing his descent from one of the very highest and most honourable titles in Ireland—a Brehon, law-giver and poet; the other brother is John Judge. In fact, hundreds of thousands of Irishmen prefer to drop their honourable Milesian names, and call themselves Groggins or Duggan, or Higgins or Guthry, or any other beastly name, in preference to the surnames of warriors, saints, and poets; and the melancholy part of it is, that not one single word of warning or remonstrance has been raised, as far as I am aware, against this colossal cringing either by the Irish public press or public men.

With our Irish Christian names the case is nearly as bad. Where are now all the fine old Irish Christian names of both men and women which were in vogue even a hundred years ago? They have been discarded as unclean things, not because they were ugly in themselves or inharmonious, but simply because they were not English. No man is now christened by a Gaelic name, "nor no woman neither." Such common Irish Christian names as Conn, Cairbre, Farfeasa, Teig, Diarmuid, Kian, Cuan, Ae, Art, Mahon, Eochaidh, Fearflatha, Cathan, Rory, Coll, Lochlainn, Cathal, Lughaidh, Turlough, Éamon, Randal, Niall, Sorley, and Conor, are now extinct or nearly so. Donough and Murrough survive in the O'Brien family. Angus, Manus, Fergal, and Felim are now hardly known. The man whom you call Diarmuid when you speak Irish, a low, pernicious, un-Irish, detestable custom, begot by slavery, propagated by cringing, and fostered by flunkeyism, forces you to call Jeremiah when you speak English, or as a concession, Darby. In like manner, the indigenous Teig is West-Britonised into Thaddeus or Thady, for no earthly reason than that both begin with a T. Donough is Denis, Cahal is Charles, Murtagh and Murough are Mortimer, Dómhnall is Daniel, Partholan, the name of the earliest coloniser of Ireland, is Bartholomew or Batty, Eoghan (Owen) is frequently Eugene, and our own O'Curry, though he plucked up courage to prefix the O to his name in later life, never discarded the Eugene, which, however, is far from being a monstrosity like most of our West-Britonised names; Félim is Felix, Finghin (Finneen) is Florence, Conor is Corney, Turlough is Terence, Éamon is Edmond or Neddy, and so on. In fact, of the great wealth of Gaelic Christian names in use a century or two ago, only Owen, Brian, Cormac, and Patrick seem to have survived in general use.

Nor have our female names fared one bit better; we have discarded them even more ruthlessly than those of our men. Surely Sadhbh (Sive) is a prettier name than Sabina or Sibby, and Nóra than Onny, Honny, or Honour (so translated simply because Nóra sounds like *onóir*, the Irish for "honour"); surely Una is prettier than Winny, which it becomes when West-Britonised. Mève, the great name of the Queen of Connacht who led the famous cattle spoiling of Cuailgne, celebrated in the greatest Irish epic, is at least as pretty as Maud, which it becomes when Anglicised, and Eibhlin (Eileen) is prettier than Ellen or Elinor. Aoife (Eefy), Sighle (Sheela), Móirin (Moreen), Nuala and Fionnuala (Finnoola), are all beautiful names which were in use until quite recently. Maurya and Anya are still common, but are not indigenous Irish names at all, so that I do not mind their rejection, whilst three other very common ones, Suraha, Shinéad, and Shuwaun, sound so bad in English that I do not very much regret their being translated into Sarah, Jane, and Joan respectively; but I must put in a plea for the retention of such beautiful words as Eefee, Oona, Eileen, Mève, Sive, and Nuala. Of all the beautiful Christian names of women which were in use a century or two ago Brighid (Breed), under the ugly form of Bridget, or still worse, of Biddy, and Eiblin under the form of Eveleen, and perhaps Norah, seem to be the only survivals, and they are becoming rarer. I *do* think that the time has now come to make a vigorous protest against this continued West-Britonising of ourselves, and that our people ought to have a word in season addressed to them by their leaders which will stop them from translating their Milesian surnames into hideous Saxon, and help to introduce Irish instead of English Christian names. As long as the Irish nation goes on as it is doing I cannot have much hope of its ultimately taking its place amongst the nations of the earth, for if it does, it will have proceeded upon different lines from every other nationality that God ever created. I hope that we shall never be satisfied either as individuals or as a society as long as the Brehonys call themselves Judges, the Clan Govern call themselves Smiths, and the O'Reardons Salmons, as long as our boys are called Dan and Jeremiah instead of Donal and Diarmuid, and our girls Honny, Winny, and Ellen instead of Nóra, Una, and Eileen.

Our topographical nomenclature too—as we may now be prepared to expect—has been also shamefully corrupted to suit English ears; but unfortunately the difficulties attendant upon a realteration of our place-names to their proper forms are very great, nor do I mean to go into this question now, for it is one so long and so difficult that it would require a lecture, or rather a series of lectures to itself. Suffice it to say, that many of the best-known names in our history and annals have become almost wholly unrecognisable, through the ignorant West-Britonising of them. The unfortunate natives of the eighteenth century allowed all kinds of havoc to be played with even their best-known names. For example the river Feóir they allowed to be turned permanently into the Nore, which happened this way. Some Englishman, asking the name of the river, was told that it was *An Fheóir*, pronounced In n'yore, because the F when preceded by the definite article *an* is not sounded, so that in his ignorance he mistook the word Feóir for Neóir, and the name has been thus perpetuated. In the same way the great Connacht lake, Loch Corrib, is really Loch Orrib, or rather Loch Orbsen, some Englishman having mistaken the C at the end of loch for the beginning of the next word. Sometimes the Ordnance Survey people make a rough guess at the Irish name and jot down certain English letters almost on chance. Sometimes again they make an Irish word resemble an English one, as in the celebrated Tailtin in Meath, where the great gathering of the nation was held, and, which, to make sure that no national memories should stick to it, has been West-Britonised Telltown. On the whole, our place names have been treated with about the same respect as if they were the names of a savage tribe which had never before been reduced to writing, and with about the same intelligence and contempt as vulgar English squatters treat the topographical nomenclature of the Red Indians. These things are now to a certain extent stereotyped, and are difficult at this hour to change, especially where Irish names have been translated into English, like Swinford and Strokestown, or ignored as in Charleville or Midleton. But though it would take the strength and goodwill of an united nation to put our topographical nomenclature on a rational basis like that of Wales and the Scotch Highlands, there is one thing which our Society can do, and that is to insist upon pronouncing our Irish names properly. Why will a certain class of people insist upon getting as far away from the pronunciation of the natives as possible? I remember a Galway gentleman pulling me up severely for speaking of Athenree. "It's not Athenree," he said, "it's called Athenrye." Yet in saying this he simply went out of his way to mispronounce the historic name, which means the "King's ford," and which all the natives call –ree, not –rye. Another instance out of many thousands is my own market town, Ballagh-ă-derreen, literally, "the way of the oak-wood." Ballach is the same word as in the phrase *Fág a' bealach*, "clear the way," and "derreen" is the diminutive of Derry, an oak-wood. Yet the more "civilised" of the population, perhaps one in fifty, offend one's ears with the frightful jargon Bálla-hád-her-een. Thus Lord Iveagh (Ee-vah) becomes Lord Ivy, and Seana-guala, the old sholder, becomes Shanagolden, and leads you to expect a mine, or at least a furze-covered hill.

I shall not give any more examples of deliberate carelessness, ineptitude, and West-Britonising in our Irish topography, for the instances may be numbered by thousands and thousands. I hope and trust that where it may be done without any great inconvenience a native Irish Government will be induced to provide for the restoration of our place-names on something like a rational basis.

Our music, too, has become Anglicised to an alarming extent. Not only has the national instrument, the harp—which efforts are now being made to revive in the Highlands—become extinct, but even the Irish pipes are threatened with the same fate. In place of the pipers and fiddlers who, even twenty years ago, were comparatively common, we are now in many places menaced by the German band and the barrel organ. Something should be done to keep the native pipes and the native airs amongst us still. If Ireland loses her music she loses what is, after her Gaelic language and literature, her most valuable and most characteristic possession. And she is rapidly losing it. A few years ago all our travelling fiddlers and pipers could play the old airs which were then constantly called for, the *Cúis d'á pléidh*, *Drinaun Dunn*, *Roseen Dubh*, *Gamhan Geal Bán*, *Eileen-a-roon*, *Shawn O'Dwyer in Glanna*, and the rest, whether gay or plaintive, which have for so many centuries entranced the Gael. But now English music-hall ballads and Scotch songs have gained an enormous place in the repertoire of the wandering minstrel, and the minstrels themselves are becoming fewer and fewer, and I fear worse and worse. It is difficult to find a remedy for this. I am afraid in this practical age to go so far as to advocate the establishment in Cork or Galway of a small institution in which young and promising pipers might be trained to play all the Irish airs and sent forth to delight our population; for I shall be told that this is not a matter for even an Irish Government to stir in, though it is certain that many a Government has lavished money on schemes less pleasant and less useful. For the present, then, I must be content with hoping that the revival of our Irish music may go hand in hand with the revival of Irish ideas and Celtic modes of thought which our Society is seeking to bring about, and that people may be brought to love the purity of

Siúbhail Siúbhail, or the fun of the *Moddereen Ruadh* in preference to "Get Your Hair Cut," or "Over the Garden Wall," or, even if it is not asking too much, of "Ta-ra-ra-boom-de-ay."

Our games, too, were in a most grievous condition until the brave and patriotic men who started the Gaelic Athletic Association took in hand their revival. I confess that the instantaneous and extraordinary success which attended their efforts when working upon national lines has filled me with more hope for the future of Ireland than everything else put together. I consider the work of the association in reviving our ancient national game of caman, or hurling, and Gaelic football, has done more for Ireland than all the speeches of politicians for the last five years. And it is not alone that that splendid association revived for a time with vigour our national sports, but it revived also our national recollections, and the names of the various clubs through the country have perpetuated the memory of the great and good men and martyrs of Ireland. The physique of our youth has been improved in many of our counties; they have been taught self-restraint, and how to obey their captains; they have been, in many places, weaned from standing idle in their own roads or street corners; and not least, they have been introduced to the use of a thoroughly good and Irish garb. Wherever the warm striped green jersey of the Gaelic Athletic Association was seen, there Irish manhood and Irish memories were rapidly reviving. There torn collars and ugly neckties hanging awry and far better not there at all, and dirty shirts of bad linen were banished, and our young hurlers were clad like men and Irishmen, and not in the shoddy second-hand suits of Manchester and London shop-boys. Could not this alteration be carried still further? Could we not make that jersey still more popular, and could we not, in places where both garbs are worn, use our influence against English second-hand trousers, generally dirty in front, and hanging in muddy tatters at the heels, and in favour of the cleaner worsted stockings and neat breeches which many of the older generation still wear? Why have we discarded our own comfortable frieze? Why does every man in Connemara wear home-made and home-spun tweed, while in the midland counties we have become too proud for it, though we are not too proud to buy at every fair and market the most incongruous cast-off clothes imported from English cities, and to wear them? Let us, as far as we have any influence, set our faces against this aping of English dress, and encourage our women to spin and our men to wear comfortable frieze suits of their own wool, free from shoddy and humbug. So shall we de-Anglicise Ireland to some purpose, foster a native spirit and a growth of native custom which will form the strongest barrier against English influence and be in the end the surest guarantee of Irish autonomy.

I have now mentioned a few of the principal points on which it would be desirable for us to move, with a view to de-Anglicising ourselves; but perhaps the principal point of all I have taken for granted. That is the necessity for encouraging the use of Anglo-Irish literature instead of English books, especially instead of English periodicals. We must set our face sternly against penny dreadfuls, shilling shockers, and still more, the garbage of vulgar English weeklies like *Bow Bells* and the *Police Intelligence*. Every house should have a copy of Moore and Davis. In a word, we must strive to cultivate everything that is most racial, most smacking of the soil, most Gaelic, most Irish, because in spite of the little admixture of Saxon blood in the north-east corner, this island *is* and will *ever* remain Celtic at the core, far more Celtic than most people imagine, because, as I have shown you, the names of our people are no criterion of their race. On racial lines, then, we shall best develop, following the bent of our own natures; and, in order to do this, we must create a strong feeling against West-Britonism, for it—if we give it the least chance, or show it the smallest quarter—will overwhelm us like a flood, and we shall find ourselves toiling painfully behind the English at each step following the same fashions, only six months behind the English ones; reading the same books, only months behind them: taking up the same fads, after they have become stale *there*, following *them* in our dress, literature, music, games, and ideas, only a long time after them and a vast way behind. We will become, what, I fear, we are largely at present, a nation of imitators, the Japanese of Western Europe, lost to the power of native initiative and alive only to second-hand assimilation. I do not think I am overrating this danger. We are probably at once the most assimilative and the most sensitive nation in Europe. A lady in Boston said to me that the Irish immigrants had become Americanised on the journey out before ever they landed at Castle Gardens. And when I ventured to regret it, she said, shrewdly, "If they did not at once become Americanised they would not be Irish." I knew fifteen Irish workmen who were working in a haggard in England give up talking Irish amongst themselves because the English farmer laughed at them. And yet O'Connell used to call us the "finest peasantry in Europe." Unfortunately, he took little care that we should remain so. We must teach ourselves to be less sensitive, we must teach ourselves not to be ashamed of ourselves, because the Gaelic people can never produce its best before the world as long as it remains tied to the apron-strings of another race and another island, waiting for *it* to move before it will venture to take any step itself.

In conclusion, I would earnestly appeal to every one, whether Unionist or Nationalist, who wishes to see the Irish nation produce its best—and surely whatever our politics are we all wish that—to set his face against this constant running to England for our books, literature, music, games, fashions, and ideas. I appeal to every one whatever his politics—for this is no political matter—to do his best to help the Irish race to develop in future upon Irish lines, even at the risk of encouraging national aspirations, because upon Irish lines alone can the Irish race once more become what it was of yore—one of the most original, artistic, literary, and charming peoples of Europe.

What Ireland is Asking for

Douglas Hyde

Translated from the original Irish. From Ideals in Ireland, compiled by Lady Gregory in 1901.

What is the chief cause that has put Ireland back now compared with other countries on this side of Europe? The answer I will give is, there are many causes, but the chief cause is – bad teaching. A country without teaching is not a real country, but a piece of earth on which a lot of people are set, without knowledge of the good beyond the bad, or of truth beyond falsehood. That is what Ireland is like. There have been schools in it for the last sixty years that have killed the mind of the country. Is there any other country in the world where we can find schoolmasters who have only one language teaching children who have only one language, and the language of the schoolmaster not the same as the language of the children? Schoolmasters "teaching" children that do not understand them, and children "learning" from masters they do not understand!

When these schools were set on foot, schools that were sarcastically given the name "National Schools," Irish was the language of the country, from Galway to Dublin, and from

Waterford to Donegal, except among the Scotch of the province of Ulster. But then masters were put to teach (or to destroy) the children who had no English, and the end of the story is that they put broken English in the place of pure Irish through three-quarters of the island. With broken English came the laying waste of the mind of a people who were as quick in speech, as quick in business, as able, as witty as any people in the whole of Europe, but were left as blind, as dull, and as dark as any wild untaught natives.

It may be thought that I am speaking too strongly on this subject. I am not adding one inch to the truth. The English schools have robbed the Gael of all that he had, – listen to the sum of things they have taken from him. In the first place, they have taken away his language, and with the language has gone his music, for they were bound together, and with his music has gone his light heart. They have taken from him his poems and his songs and his old sayings and his stories, and they have taken away his knowledge of the history of his country and of his forefathers, for they, too, were bound up with the language, and when it was taken from him they went also. They have taken from him his wit and his quickness and his deep thinking, for he can never bring out the deep things that are in him in the broken English that has been put in his mouth; and the man that is without stories, without music, without poems, without traditions, without knowledge of the history of his country and of his own forefathers – it is not usual for that man to have any thought at all, except the trivial thoughts that come to him from the wants of the hour. This is how Ireland and the Irish are left now, and it is little wonder that the people should be so backward and so ignorant as they are.

And it is not only the poor people who have suffered like this, but big people in the same way. If an Irishman were as learned as a Chief Olamh in all the things that related to Ireland and the Irish, there was not a penny of profit to be got out of that knowledge. Everything was banished that belonged to Ireland, and the Gael out of the lower schools and out of the high schools and out of the colleges. Nothing was taught but things that did not belong to Ireland, things that were of special interest to the English, or things that were common to the whole world. No one could think it possible to build up an intelligent people on that road – but men with no knowledge of the human mind. It is not in such a manner that other countries teach. A friend of mine was in Denmark, and he was astonished at the amount of wealth got out of so poor a country by dairies and by farming. "No doubt," said my friend to a well-educated Dane, "the children are instructed in the schools as to dairying and farming."

"They are not," said the Dane, "but they are taught the old Danish poems (sagas) in the schools; that makes good Danes of the children, and then they become good farmers."

That is a true word!

Our Commissioners of Education have succeeded in making bad Irishmen by millions, but they have never succeeded, and they never will succeed, by their method in making good farmers of them.

There are now a hundred and fifty branches of the Gaelic League, and it is the sure belief of everyone who is in them that Ireland will always be backward until every Irishmen learns to have respect for himself and, as well as that, love for his country. "Respect for ourselves and love for our country" – that is the grip for the people to raise themselves with. We are all convinced that they will never raise themselves without that. And there are educated men amongst us that came from the people, and that live among the people, and that know the people twenty times better than the lords and gentlemen who sit on the National Board, and everyone of them knows that this is the truth.

Now, what is the cure for this mischief? What is there for us to do to make the Irishman respected again, himself and his children? It is, the Gaelic League says, to change the teaching, and teach Irish-wise henceforth and not English-wise. In any place where the old tongue is living, teach through the old tongue, and in any place where it is dead, allow the people to learn it, if they desire it. Teach the history of Ireland to the children of Ireland. Give liberty to every school to teach history if it chooses, to teach its own choice of history; not a tasteless, feeble, history, but a popular history that will have sap and pleasure in it, a history that will take a grip of the child. It is an abuse beyond bounds that there should be a man on the Board who will not allow Irish history to be read in any school unless it teaches lies, unless it teaches the children that their forefathers that came before them were naked savages, without learning, without character, without any sort of good behaviour. That man would now allow Irish children to learn Irish history unless the history contains falsehoods like this. This shows he has never given any heed to human nature. If you take a young boy, a boy who has come from a gentle and honourable stock, and if you put in his head that his father was but a tinker and that his mother was but a beggar woman, do you think you increase that boy's honour or his respect for himself, or that you make his conduct or his behaviour better, or that you do him any good at all? No good ever came of a lie, but miserable harm will come of a lie of this sort. The rock that is the foundation-stone of the Gaelic League is "The Irish mind" and "Respect for our race," and if this is allowed to us we will build up some certain thing upon it; but the people of the Board wanted in the past to make their own hovel on a wet bog, and without any stone foundation under it, but contempt of the people for themselves, and contempt for and ignorance of their race. They will never rear anything till the day of

Judgment on their rotten foundations, but a thing without strength, without goodness, without profit, not to be put in comparison with the building of other countries. The greater share of those who are directing the education of the Irish are politicians; their teaching was intended to throw education back, and their desire was not to make an understanding people of the Irish, but to make them an Englishised people. And with the hope of making them good Englishmen in the end, they began by making bad Irishmen of them, and that is a bad beginning.

There is Irish teaching wanted in this country, and the country itself has this long time been calling on the Board to give it. The Catholic Bishops ask for it, the managers of twelve hundred schools ask for it, the hundred and fifty branches of the Gaelic League ask for it, the County Councils and Rural Councils in their hundreds ask for it, but they have not got it.

There is no free country in the whole of Christendom where, if the people of the country asked such a thing as this with one will and one voice, as has been done in Ireland, it would not be given at once as a matter of course. But it is not so in Ireland. If there is any little thing we want in this country we have to begin to wrangle and to make a disturbance and put fights and tumults on foot, much as the English would have to do if they wanted to disestablish the House of Lords. And yet people tell us that this is a free country! The National Board is not under the authority of Parliament itself, and the whole nation has asked it to give us sensible Irish teaching, and we are none the better off. It is not possible for us to ask more strongly than we have asked. There is nothing else we can do without breaking the peace. And people still say this is a free country!

The high schools and colleges of Ireland are now doing their very best to build up people in the likeness of the people who are brought up in England. But if they will think for a moment they will see their folly.

We do not agree by any means that the same education that suits the English suits also the Irish, and it is not in our mind that an English education is better than an Irish one for Irish boys. If all who are brought up in these schools were to go to England when they grow up, or to make their home among Englishmen, it would be possible to think there was some little right on the side of the directors of these schools; but when it is sure and certain that the greater part of them will stay at home in Ireland itself, or go amongst their kinsmen in America, then we must be dissatisfied at seeing them without the Irish education that is fitting for them.

If I am asked what is an Irish education, I would say that it is one that teaches the student, as a matter of course, everything that relates to Ireland and the Irish before teaching things relating to England and the English. I would say that if people are to live all their life in Ireland (as most of us are) it is much more necessary to them to have a knowledge of things relating to Ireland, the place where they are going to live, than of things relating to England, where they are not going to live. This is according to nature, and I do not think there is another country in the world where this truth is forgotten as it is here.

I do not think there is any other country in the world where the men who are in charge of the education of the people are not accountable either to the people or to the Government; nor do I think there is any other country in the world where the riches, and the endowments, and the treasures of learning, that belong to the country, are left in the keeping of men so blinded with politics and with religious bigotry as are the greater share of the learned men in "that English fort," Trinity College.

ABOUT THE EDITOR

Keith Woods is an Irish author, publisher, public speaker and activist. He is the author of *Nationalism: The Politics of Identity*. Originally a popular vlogger and social media personality, his newsletter, keithwoods.pub, is one of the most widely read political Substacks in the world. He has also contributed to the Unz Review and Counter-Currents.

Printed in Great Britain
by Amazon